My Boys

a collection of poems

Melbourne Peat

authorHOUSE®

AuthorHouse™
1663 Liberty Drive
Bloomington, IN 47403
www.authorhouse.com
Phone: 1-800-839-8640

First published by AuthorHouse   7/19/2011

ISBN: 978-1-4567-6917-8 (sc)
ISBN: 978-1-4567-6918-5 (e)

Library of Congress Control Number: 2011908338

Printed in the United States of America

Contents

PLAY GRANDPA, PLAY

Play Grandpa. Play Grandpa.
Nice Grandpa. Nice grandpa.
Dancing feet took a hold of me.

My God,
Joy took a hold of me.

My Boy,
Those words will take me to the grave.

How could I not love my blood?
The young and old find a bundle of joy.
True love, my boy, will never die.
I beg of you,
Spread the legacy.
Take my hands to the heart of man.

My Boy,
Use your mind to focus on that which is good.

Love always,
Grandpa Melbourne Peat

WORDS

My Boy,
They don't know what words mean to me.
Words set my soul on fire.
I said fire to lift my spirit.
Without words, I would be dead to reasoning.
How could I poke fun in the face of suffering?

My Boy,
If I had not committed my hands for the good of man,
The burden of man would escape mine eyes.

My Boy,
Without words, how could I share?
The time spent alone would be a waste.
Sweet words, my boy, are like music to the heart.

THE EARTH

My God,
When the earth burst,
Man was no match for its belly.
Faces that were once filled with hatred,
Now dripping tears like raindrops.

My God, My God,
How long could the hands of hatred last?
Yes, man, confront the hands of the Great Ruler.
The hoarding of fine gold lines the frames of the dead.
Fire moves everything in its path.
A nation is under the spell of disaster.
Now its people are crying out to God.

BEAUTIFUL

My Boy,
Love can be beautiful.
Sweet sleep will allow dreams their course.
A rested man will find his spirit on a high note.
It's better to find the joy of true love than carry the pain of hatred.
A loving man will be free with his hands.
In this time of great hardship,
What the world needs is some free hands.
Only true love will free up the hands.

A GIFT OF LOVE

My Boy,
You have given the best gift a man could ask for,
A bundle of love that will outlive me.
What joy I have found.

My Boy,
I am a new man now.
It's my duty to spread the love.
For the good of man,
I shall coin words to heal the troubled souls.

THE HANDS OF JUSTICE

My God,
Her little body was no match for the hands of evil.
A father filled with rage cast her to the mercy of the river.

My God,
A nation witnessed evil at its core.
A father could not find time to have mercy.

My God,
At this hour tears find my wrath.
May her young soul find favor with thee.
Awake, my spirit.
Awake, my spirit.
I have seen man gone mad.

Lord,
The working of the mind I cannot understand.
What kind of heart is he fitted with?
A young child could not get the time to bloom.

Blessed Father,
Today I come before you a broken man.
My spirit cannot rest.
Let the hands of justice take its course.

DEATH

How could I not weep for my beloved,
When death came for her in a hurry?
Now that she is on her journey,
May the angels await her.

My Lord,
Heaven-bound I pray.

My Dear,
You have lived a pleasing life.
May the living take heed.
May your work speak for you.

MAN AND BOY

My Friends,
Come look at our eyes.
Man and boy bonding for the first time.
He is my blood.
How could I not love him?

My Friends,
Hide not your eyes.
The meeting of the minds is on display.
How I had longed for this day.
Look at my hands.
If only eyes could talk.
Man and boy find love at first sight.

My God,
You have seen our paths.
May your hands be our guides.
Today I have seen my heart's desire.
Let no man take away what is mine.
Let me live to give of myself.
Fine gold have I none.
Yet I come with a song of love.

I SHALL BE WITH YOU

My Boy,
I shall be with you in spirit.
Your young mind shall wonder who I am.
Do not be afraid.
It's me, not a stranger.
It's me, your Grandpa,
A man from a far away land,
A man who came to this land for a purpose.

SWEET LOVE

Sweet Love,
Come to me that I may taste of thee.
Let no man take away what is yours.
When a man is called to rejoice with his clapping hands,
The good God must have sanctioned his move.

Sweet Love,
To the watching eyes, let them be fixed.
Come to me that I may taste of thee.

BOAST NOT

My Friends,
Boast not of your standing.
I have seen the fall of man.
That shame took a hold of him.
In his lowest form,
Madness took over his head.
It is better to humble thyself.

My Friends,
Watch and pray.
Be thankful to see another day.
Along life's journey,
May peace be upon you.
Remember: A good deed is expected of you.

SPEAK TO HIM

My Dear,
What sorrows can we share?
The suffering man cannot escape.
Well, then, fold not your hands.
Use them to wash away the dirt.
Man in a state of madness crying out.

My Dear,
Let us lend a helping hand.
Speak to him from your heart.
Lend him a mother's heart.

TRUE LOVE

My Dear,
I lift my hands to love.
Strong love, my dear, is like music to the soul.
A happy heart is better than fine gold.
Only death can stop its rhythm.

My Dear,
Don't forget the lover's wings.

My Dear,
If all the tears drip and you cannot find this hand,
Let the wings be fitted.

A TRAVELLING SON

My people, if I do not return to the land of my birth,
Forget not your son.
Even though the womb from which I came now returns to the land,
My spirit cannot rest.
From my adopted home I shall share my tears.
This land has been good to me.
When I was hungry for knowledge,
They prepared a place for me.
I am who I am because of so many good hands.

My people, for the love of humanity,
I pray you spread the wealth.
Out of many, let us be thankful.
We are all God's children.

My people, waste not the hands of your traveling son.

A SONG OF LOVE

My Boy,
When I remember how David played upon his harp to please his Lord,
Who am I not to play for you?
A joyful heart is upon me.

My Boy,
You are the first.
You came, you looked and you smiled.
From the lips of others came a song of victory.
Who could it be but the working of the Lord?
Before their very eyes,
Man and boy seal their love.

My Boy,
Today I am with the mountain.
With this hand I shall honor thee.
Play Grandpa, play Grandpa.
Nice Grandpa, nice Grandpa.

My Boy,
If it pleases your heart.
May this day be in remembrance of thee.
Sweet Lord, under the face of the sun,
I lifted my eyes towards your secret place.
Let me please the heart of this boy.
May the words I string together be upon his lips for the good of man.

May 18, 2009

GRANDSON POEM

My Boy,
You are the first.
If I teach you well,
My years should be a part of your thinking.
For the good of man,
I shall ask of thee,
Go to your roots and look at their hands.
As for me,
I have trained these for you.
If only fingers could talk.
This moment in time, I pray.
Blessed Father, for the good of man,
I present this boy to thee.
Lead him that he may follow the path of the Good Shepherds.

My Boy,
When I remember your eyes,
The work to be done is a must.
Remember that we are all God's children.
Forget not your fallen brothers and sisters.
Give unto them the food they need.
When I remember the hands of my ancestors,
I say to myself, how could they be so free with their hands?
Now that I am of age,
I have seen the light.
The fear of God and the love for humanity took a hold of them.

My Boy,
Go and do your work.
Forget not your human face.

May 23, 2009

DREAM ON

If I should cry, please do not leave my tears dripping.
Let your hands work for me.
Talk with me that my ears lift to thee.
A man laden with heavy burdens will beg for mercy.
Along life's journey, no one can predict the future.
My friends, if a man dresses with dignity, he will find the
sweetness in life.
A simple life would be a blessing.
Today as I look at man in another house,
What sorrows have I seen?

Father, help me to deal with the pain and pleasure.
Sometimes up, sometimes down.
The rise and fall of man is a part of his destiny.
Oh! Troubled man, do not get weary.
Make use of your knees.
Go into your heart and remove the dirt.
Dress yourself in courage and press on.
Dream on, my brother.
Everything will be all right.

May 27, 2009

THE HIGHEST PRINCIPLES

My Friends,
If you cannot strive for the highest principles towards the suffering man,
Do not apply within.
The pain will be too much for you.
In this house,
Man and his troubled mind will feed upon your very soul.
Well, then, allow me to continue.

Power higher than I,
Let me find the conscience to be human.
My Lord,
Pulling eyes excites the hardest of hearts.
As I rise to meet the eyes of the troubled man,
Help me to stand firm.
For the good of man,
Give unto me comforting words.
My Lord,
Help me to dress in the moral principle of love.
A loving heart will find that which is good.
Blessed Father,
It is well with me.
Spur me that I may continue to run for the good of man.

June 5, 2009

ALLOW LOVE TO OVERCOME EVIL

My Boy,
Allow love to overcome evil.
On the morality of man,
I pray that you will find wisdom.

My Boy,
If you can bring a smile to a face,
Harden not your heart.
It is better to love than to hate.
A heart that is full with hatred is not good for the soul.

My Boy,
Use your young eyes to look at human nature.
I have seen man possessed with greed,
Then trade his soul for earthly treasures.
A fool sitting on golden seats,
Not knowing how long it will last.

I have seen the hearse taking the rich and the poor along.
The earth with its open mouth awaits what is left.
Who is man that I should be mindful of?
Here today and tomorrow, nowhere to be found.

June 9, 2009

COME AGAIN

My Lady, just to make sure,
My lonely days are few.
Your eyes, I had no choice but to keep.
I saw something good in you.
If I had not controlled myself,
This heart would have leapt to thee.
What fire you brought with you.
I do not know why I am on fire.

My Lady, bring me water.
If I should live,
All I will do is pray.
Come again that I may drink from the Fountain of Love.

June 10, 2009

I CANNOT REST

When morning comes, I cannot rest.
The burden of the suffering man made a bed in my chest.
Why should I fatten myself when he is begging for bread?
Have I not eyes to see how far he is gone?
How can I love myself if I cannot give of myself?
Father, help me to work upon my calling.
If I cannot find my heart, the true meaning of love will not be found.
My Father, if I can work for the benefit of humanity, help me to feed
upon that which is good.
Even though fine gold have I none, the work must go on.
Let me find the courage to face the suffering man.
Awake, my spirit.
Awake, my spirit.
The time is right for the good of man.
Blessed Father, if only I can find the spirit of your light, my path would
be clear as crystal.
With this hand I beg of thee.

June 10, 2009

SENDING MY THOUGHTS

My Boy,
Today the rain is upon me.
I have no choice but to be still.
Let me allow my thoughts to find thee.
If I allow true love to set sail upon the waters,
Your destination I shall reach.
If my heart cries for thee,
Your eyes I will need.
For the good of man,
I seek your young hands.
Nothing in this world, my boy, will slow me down.
The faith I have in you,
I shall work this hand to bare bones.
Your youthfulness, my boy, is a blessing.
Help me to continue on the journey.
Everyday I pray for your young hands.

Blessed Father,
You have seen this boy.
Let him find the path of the Good Shepherds.
Let him be true to himself that he may find the heart for the good of man.

June 10, 2009

A LITTLE BOY

The voice of a little boy,
Play for me, too.
Play for me, too.
How could I not play for that little face?

My child, your little voice caught my ears.
Peace and love, my child.
I shall love you just as my own.
My child, when I am called,
Who am I not to do the Father's work?
We are all God's children.
True love, my child, shall find true love.
Sweet songs I shall find for thee.
Blessed Father, you have seen the young souls.
May the elders give unto them that which is good.
Today I have seen a happy child.

June 10, 2009

AS I PRAY

Blessed Father, today I come to thee from the mountain.
I shall ask of thee as I await the face of the sun.
I call upon thee for the food I need.
Comforting words, my Lord, would be a blessing.
For the good of man, let me be true.
With this hand, let me pull from within.
Help me to unwrap this heart of mine.
The voice of the suffering man will not leave.
Father, all I can do is pray.
As I pray, show me the way that I may lead.

June 10, 2009

ALLOW MY EYES

You said you love me.
Yet your eyes I cannot find.
What strange love have I seen.
Today I shall dress myself to give of my hands.
My love, I shall come with clean hands.
Oh! Take me that I may be well again.
Give unto me the fire I need.
If I could only find the right path,
My steps would be sweet.
Oh! Sweet love, hide not your face.
Allow my eyes to be full

June 12, 2009

BEFORE I WRITE

My Boy,
Before I write, I set my heart upon peace.
Then set myself in a near trance.
Hidden words I then seek to find.
When I remember the suffering man,
I try to reason with a higher source.

My Boy,
To find good food, it takes time.
A man needs patience to wait upon his Lord.
If I cry out for words,
It's because my mind is bent on doing good.

June 12, 2009

TIME WILL TELL

Follow me, my brother.
You and I shall walk hand in hand.
Today for the good of man,
Justice and only justice shall be our cry.
Rise up, my brother.
Let your voice be heard.
Stand and face the music.
Be true to yourself.
Let no man take away what is yours.
Set your heart upon that which is good,
Then allow time to work things out.

June 12, 2009

LET ME FIND YOUR HANDS

My Friends,
Come, let us keep watch.
This is no place for the weak heart.
Man and his evil self have exposed his evil hands.
If you cannot stand firm,
Put on your running shoes.
Well, then, let me speak.
The working of the mind is beyond my control.
Sweet words I cannot find.
Father, you have seen man and how he is gone.
As I cry to thee,
Leave me not.
My brothers and sisters stand with me.
I and I shall move forward.
For the good of man,
Let me find your hands.

June 13, 2009

SWEET SLEEP

Sweet sleep, my dear.
This old lion cannot rest.
In the House of Pain, I stand at the gates of the suffering man.
My Lord, my Lord, what sorrows I have seen.
Today, today I beg for your mercy.
Even though my heart is full, my mind is bent on doing good.
How can I turn my back when the work must be done?
For the good of man, let me see the light.

June 13, 2009

FIRE SET BY HATRED

Awake, my soul.
Awake, my soul.
The eyes of man are on fire.
I said fair set by hatred.
What on earth drove him to such madness?

Blessed Father,
You have seen this man.
What shall I do?
If only I could find the courage to tap his mind.
His eyes and mine would be fixed.

Father,
Help me that I may go forth.
I cannot leave now.
In the name of humanity,
I beg for thy hands.
Let me find the right words to cool his anger.

Father,
Without you I am nothing.
In Your name all things are possible.
I am bent on moving forward.

July 21, 2009

PEACE AND LOVE

My Boy,
At this hour on your birthday,
My thoughts are upon you.
Let me pray.

Father,
In your name I present this boy,
A boy so loving that he attracted the eyes of many.
Even though young at heart,
I will not rest until I find that one poem for you to carry.
The words, my boy,
Use them for the heart of man.
Year by year I pray that you will return to the well.
Refresh your spirit,
Then continue on your journey.

My Boy,
The task laid out for you will not be easy,
But I have seen something good in you.
You are among the peacemakers.

July 22, 2009

A FREE SPIRIT

My Dear,
Mine eyes allow mine heart to suffer.
What temptations the power of love breeds.

My Dear,
If my soul finds the freedom to fight for this love,
A sweet heart I shall bring to the game.
I shall not allow the sun to set before the game is over.
A free spirit will come to thee.

July 23, 2009

IN THE NAME OF LOVE

My Boy,
You and I are a product of July.
Only God knows why.
So many years apart,
Yet we find a common ground.
An old man and a little boy showing what is love.
No amount of hands could stop the praying hands.
Who is man to stand in the path of the Father?

My Boy,
I shall call upon you to let us unite.
Unity, my boy, in the name of love will heal a nation.

July 25, 2009

ALL IS WELL

Before my very eyes,
The true meaning of love came to life.
A boy at the break of dawn,
Showering his love to heal a broken heart.
The spirit of the Most High was upon him.
My friends, come rejoice with me.
All is well.
All is well with me.

July 26, 2009

PURE LOVE

My Boy,
When a man finds pure love,
His heart served him well.
His spirit will attract others.
Peace and only peace will be upon his lips.

My Boy,
It is better to love than hate.

My Boy,
Hatred is not good for the face.
What rage, what madness engulf the soul of a man full of hatred.

My Boy,
A peaceful man will transmit true love.
His heart will be at ease.
His face will attract others.

July 26, 2009

COME, MY BOY

Come, my boy,
Let us speak of true love.
Oh! Lord, in your name I pray.
The soul of a young boy and the soul of an old man find peace.
True love, my boy, generates peace.
For the love of humanity,
We shall carry the light.

My Boy,
I come to you a grown man,
A man of many years.
If I cannot bring you comfort,
Why should I open mine eyes?
The teaching of our great Father is built upon love.
Who am I not to follow?
I will not allow pride to excite this heart.

My Boy,
We shall walk hand in hand knowing that I will be stronger.
Come, my boy, come follow me.
If I teach you well,
May I rest in peace.
One love, one heart, peace be unto you, my boy.

July 26, 2009

I SHALL GIVE THANKS

My Boy,
On my birthday I shall await the sun.
I shall give thanks to the Most High for another year.
The working of the mine I shall put to use for the good of man.

Oh! Heavenly Father,
You have seen this man.
The sun I cannot find, yet I await.
Dark clouds, my Lord, are all I see.

Father,
What's going on in this land is more than I.
The suffering of man brings tears to the eyes.
A great nation fell upon bad times.
Man feeding upon greed fattens his own heart.

My Lord, My Lord,
When will it end?
As I watch the moving of the clouds,
Heaven-bound I pray.

Father,
You provided for the birds.
Why should many worry?
As for me, I shall await thy hands.
Help me to work this mind for the good of man.
If I can bring joy to one weary soul,
My years upon this land would be sweet.
Today, today with sun upon me,
Father, help me to follow the light.

July 26, 2009

PLAYING WITH WORDS

Before you lay me down,
My hands are already devoted to my soul.
The fingers of an ordinary man cleaning his soul.
The purpose of the human mind will not escape the raw emotions.
What I am shall be who I am.
If I belong to you in spirit,
Show me your motion.
I have enough pain in the brain.
There is no room for garbage.
The hands of an ordinary man are at work.
No fool will lay me down.
My heart is like an old lion.
I harbor in silence for the good of man.
If you find my words to be dark and deep,
Heap no shame upon me.
My heart is before your eyes.
Focus on helping the suffering man.
The old lion has set the stage.

July 26, 2009

BIRTHDAYS

My Boy,
Your birthday and mine are days apart.
We are both a product of July.
The old and the young finding a common ground.
Today I shall celebrate yours and mine together.

Blessed Father,
Today I come to you a humble man.
With these knees I present my boy and I to thee.
May we live to see many more years.

Father,
This is the old lion, a product of July.
On this day of my birth,
I took time out to write for my boy and I.
Peace, my Lord, I bring to my brothers and sisters.
Let the love the boy and I share serve as a mirror for mankind.
Let the lips of man jump with comforting words.

My Boy,
Let true love be true love.

July 26, 2009

TO BE LOVED

My Dear,
What pleasure thy love brings to me.
Moving feet I cannot control.
Sweet laughter calling my spirit.
A hungry man will run to find food.
A thirsty man will seek water.
A man seeking love will run ahead to find what is good for his heart.
No fear shall stop his light feet.
To be loved is the dream of every living soul.
Man finding love will taste the sweetness of his heart.

July 26, 2009

THIS LAND

My Boy,
This land of yours, I shall not leave.
Dreams, my Boy, I shall follow.
For the good of man, I cannot rest.
My mind is set to follow the path of the Good Shepherds.

My Boy,
On my journey I shall leave marks for you.
My hands will be my trademark.
As I pray, may your young hands pick up the pieces.
Let no man put you down.
Stand firm and fight for a just cause.

July 26, 2009

IF I

My Friends,
If I cannot use this hand for the good of man,
Why should I be allowed to use it?
Well, then, at this hour I am confronted with the burden of man.
What madness I have seen.
Oh! Great Father, you have seen the fall of man.
A mind that once shaped good reasoning,
Now at a loss to find words.
Father, help me to find a way to reach this soul.
Even though afraid, I shall move forward.
I shall face the plight of man with a human face.
Who am I?
What am I?
The work must be done.
My Lord, my Lord, why me?
The pain and pleasure I pray to endure.

July 28, 2009

GO TO THE MOUNTAIN

My Dear,
Feeling love is just right for the heart.
No more tears.
No more sorrows.
Working lips on the move.

My Dear,
It is sweet to be in love.

My Friends,
Go to the mountain and be alive again.

July 29, 2009

COME, MY BOY

My Boy,
When I heard the news, my heart leapt for joy.
True love, my Boy, I shall feed upon.
Blessed Father, you have seen the desire of this heart.
One the subject of love,
Let us, as people, share that inner feeling.

My Boy,
Let me pray.
Heavenly Father, in this mindset, I beg of thee.
Teach me thy ways.
Let me find the path to the Fountain of Love.
Come, my Boy, come follow me.

July 30, 2009

LEAN ON YOUR FAITH

My Boy,
When hardship arrives,
Lean on your faith.
Talk with God and find that comfort.

My Boy,
In time of great need,
Friends will leave you on the wayside.

My Boy,
Faith means everything.
Magnify the name of the great Creator.
Through him all things are possible.
Hardship or no hardship, he will be there.
Prepare your thoughts,
Then find time to reason with the Most High.

My Boy,
Forget not to lean on your faith.

July 30, 2009

DRIPPING TEARS

My Dear,
In every drip of tears,
There goes a drip of love.
How long, my dear, shall I await thee?
Have I not sent for thee?
Come to me.
Come to me.
Let true love be true love.

July 30, 2009

WHAT BEAUTY

My Dear,
I have seen something good in you.
What beauty have I seen?

My Lady, for the good of man I beg of thee.
Let your light shine.
Come to me.
Come and let us unite.
Your hands I shall seek to find.
If I had not seen something good in you,
My spirit would not find what I need.

My Lady,
Let us be true to ourselves.

July 30, 2009

THE NEWS

My Boy,
When I got the call,
I said to my soul, "Come let us go and see my blood."
At the break of dawn the moon and stars were my guiding light.
My lips moving words to the God I served.
Oh! What a blessed day.

My Boy,
Nothing beats prayers.
Clearance, my boy, was upon the land.
You and I fixing our eyes.

My Boy,
You are a part of who I am.
How could we not find love?

My God,
May we never forget this morning.
May the eyes that witness the working of the Lord,
Use their lips to spread the news.

August 2, 2009

LET HIM RISE

The voice of a boy crying out.
I love the water.
My Boy, that water is the holy water.
My boy, you will be all right.
The hands of man leading you to the Holy Father.
Blessed Father, today this boy is before you.
Grant unto him peace.
May his heart be that of a loving child.
Father, before these eyes, let him rise for the good of man.

August 3, 2009

THE FACE

My God,
The face of madness is too much for the heart.
What evil spell I have seen.

Father,
You have seen your creation,
Man in a state of rage.

Father,
What should I do?
Help me to stand firm.

August 4, 2009

THE DREAMER

My Love,
When I leave,
Dream of me with pure happiness.
Alone I shall allow sweet sleep to hold me down.
My nights shall be yours.
At the break of dawn,
I shall leave to find thee.
I shall learn the art of true love.
I pray that sweet dreams will shed some light,
A light that I will be able to follow

My Love,
What passion pulls this heart.
Help the dreamer dream along.

August 4, 2009

TEACH HIM

My Boy,
I shall stand in the presence of man.
Then speak to thee.
How could I not share the love?
Man and boy finding a common ground.

My Boy,
God takes are of His people.
Let you and me rise up for the good of man.
Let the old and young minds unite.
Good love we shall share.
As I follow the hands of time,
I will not give sleep to these eyes.
Duty, my boy, I shall keep watch.
Words, my boy, I shall find for your lips.
I beg of you,
Take them to the heart of man.
Teach him the way to love.

August 4, 2009

LET HIM BE PROUD

My Boy,
At night I cannot sleep.
The work must be done.
I cannot await many more years.
Time awaits no man.
The music from within I shall bring forth.
Upon this pillow my head cannot rest.
Full moon took over my window.
My thoughts I shall put in order.
Words, my boy, I shall put a little sugar.
Sweet words I shall leave for you.

My Boy,
Remember the children.
Remember life is beautiful.
Live and let others live.

My Boy,
If you find the teaching of the old man sound,
Let him be proud.

August 5, 2009

DRIPPING TEARS

My Dear,
In every drip of tears goes a drip of love.
How long, my dear, shall I await thee?
Have I not sent for thee?
Come to me.
Come to me.
Let true love be true love.
Oh, what eyes have I carried!

August 5, 2009

THE BOY AND HIS SONG

The song of a boy.
Play Grandpa. Play Grandpa.
Nice Grandpa. Nice Grandpa.
These words flow from the heart of a child.
The good God must have touched him.
A little boy singing to please the heart of his Grandpa.
Oh! What a day, such a glorious day.
The meeting of the minds in full sight.
Oh, witness, go and speak the truth!
Man and boy sharing their love,
A love made in heaven.
Only God knows the true meaning.

My Boy,
Come, let us go and do our Father's work.
My Boy,
Let no man take away what is yours.
Let the goodness of your heart speak to the eyes of man.

August 5, 2009

A COMMAND TO THE SOUL

My Boy,
I said to my soul, "Let true love stay within its confines."
My Boy,
If I weep for joy,
Do not be ashamed.
The power of love is upon me.
Oh! What a precious gift.
Come, let us go to the heart of man.

August 5, 2009

TODAY

If a man cannot find time to reason,
Why should he live?
Life and its journey will not be easy.
Well, then, today I took time out to reason with the Great Master.
Even though the sun is on me,
I shall not be removed from the East.
The winds came,
And I am delighted by dancing trees.

My Friends,
What beauty nature has to offer.
Birds upon birds fine tuning their songs.
What sweet melodies grace my ears.

My Lord, My Lord,
Today, today I come before you.

Blessed Father,
I am on my journey.
This land is not my home.
Let me stay before the good of man.
I have seen man strapped with madness.
That I cannot rest.

Father,
If only I could understand the working of the mind.
My years would be sweet.

Father,
I am ready for your teaching.
The return of man I pray.

August 5, 2009

A LOOK AT GREED

My Boy,
I shall look at greed.
A few fat cats pulling out the souls of the poor.
Man who lines his soul with fine gold makes a mockery of the
suffering man.

My God,
How long shall it last?
When will it end?
For the love of humanity,
I pray for some good souls.
The love for humanity is a must.

Father,
We are all your children.
Let the poor find a way to drink from the well.
A thirsty man cannot find peace.
His thoughts will be too much for him to control.

August 5, 2009

THE EYES OF EVIL

When you look into the eyes of evil,
What fear comes to light?
When a man allows his soul to follow the path of hatred,
All eyes will be upon him.
Life is too short to play a fool.
Man, rise up and follow the path of good.

August 5, 2009

MY BOY, LET ME SPEAK

My Boy,
Today I am in a state of readiness.
My heart I have purified.
I shall now speak to thee.
Use your young mind to fashion that which is good.

My Boy,
Seek and find the teaching of the elders.
Let your journey be for the good of man.

My Boy,
Call upon your God to come along.
As for me, today I am with the mountain.

My Boy,
My spirit cannot rest.
The work must be done.
The weight I will not allow to beat me down.
The working of the mind I shall put to use.
For the good of man,
I shall train these thoughts.
Half-naked or not,
The work must be done.

Great Father,
You have seen the desire of this heart.
Help me to find the food I need.
Oh! Young mind, come with me.
Let us go and find the heart of the children.

My Boy,
If you feed a child with that which is good,
Such a child will produce that which is good.

August 5, 2009

THROUGH YOUR EYES

My Boy,
I shall look at love through your eyes.
It takes a child to teach the elders what love is.
An innocent mind finds the time to love,
A love without any strings attached.

My Boy,
You are an instrument of peace.
The good Lord must have sent you to heal a nation.
A loving family is what this nation needs.

My Boy,
I shall dedicate my years spreading the words.
A creative purpose I shall develop.
The spring of love I shall drink from.

My People,
Where there is hatred, let there be love.
Great faith, my boy, I shall follow.

August 5, 2009

A POET SEEKING WORDS

A poet seeking words will find a place to invite his God.
Alone he will reason in silence.
The love for humanity will be a burden to his heart.
In his mind something must be done.
The searching of the heavens will consume his thoughts.
Something must be done for the good of man.
A poet speaking with his God will beg for words.
Comforting words will be upon him.
Man and his troubled mind cannot stand alone.
Food for his growth will be the cry of the poet.
Yes, let I and I find the time to weep.
For the love of humanity, let me pray.
Blessed Father, let me find the words I need.
The eyes of man await my hands.

August 5, 2009

A POEM OF LOVE

A poem of love.
Come my love.
Come my love.
Let us find a place to rest.
Let the gladness of our hearts be magnified.
In the name of true love,
Let us seal our years.
Let us find our knees and give thanks.
Let those with eyes feed upon that which is good.
Come let us go now for the world to see.

August 5, 2009

WORKING UPON A DREAM

My Boy,
I shall allow dignity to shape my destiny.
The teaching of my parents served as bedrock.
Their hands were laid upon my youthfulness.

Boy,
Go to school, then find your calling.
Forget not the poor.
You have seen you mother and I.
No one shall turn away from this house hungry.

Well, then, my boy,
We expect you to follow our teaching.
Today I shall honor the love I received.
May God help me to find the heart to fulfill a dream.

August 5, 2009

THIS HEAD

My Boy,
This head will not cease to honor thee.
My years I shall use to guide thee.
When I remember my father and his grandfather.

My Boy,
I lift my hat to thee.

My Boy,
You are on the right road.
I pray that you will find many years.

My Boy,
It is in your breeding to do good.
Let your ancestors be proud.
As for me, I shall leave no stone unturned.
The teaching of my Father I shall share with you.

My Boy,
You will be the leader one day.
Do not wash yourself in tears.
Go and study the elders.
Then put into practice what you learn.

My Boy,
Do not be afraid.
I have seen something good in you.

August 5, 2009

ON MY JOURNEY

My Boy,
I am on my journey.
If I do not follow the path of good,
How will I find the Good Shepherds?
A warm and loving heart I shall cultivate.
Life is short and I shall play my part.

High praises I shall not seek.
A good name is upon my mind.
Let me pray.

Blessed Father.
Let me come to you.

August 5, 2009

TIME WILL TELL

My Boy,
I shall share my thoughts to fit your young mind,
Even though too young to understand.

My Boy,
Time will tell.
History will look upon this hand.
My stay upon this land will be for the good of man.
I will not allow fine gold to blind these eyes.
I have seen the hearse taking man without his earthly gains.

Well, then, my Boy,
I shall take heed.
I shall not dwell upon vanity.
The working of the mind I shall use for the good of man.

My Boy,
I shall carry no human fear.
The road I choose is a must.
If I become too weak,
Help me along.

August 5, 2009

THIS LOVE

My Boy,
If I cannot express this love with all my heart,
Something is wrong with me.
To tell you it's me, look for the words, my Boy.

My Boy,
You brought a fresh spirit to this heart,
A spirit that stimulates the mind,
A mind that I shall use to spread love.
As I await the sun,
There is no room for hatred.
Life is short and the work must be done.

My Boy,
I have to prepare the foundation for you to build upon.
With these old hands I shall toil night and day.

My Boy,
The real world is short of love.
War upon war driving man to madness.

My Boy,
Peace and love I pray.
With your young mind,
Use it for the good of man.

Blessed Father,
As I craft these words,
May this boy find the food he needs.

August 7, 2009

THE RHYTHM OF LOVE

My Boy,
I shall allow this heart to beat upon love.
Sweet songs I shall sing.

My Boy,
Singing a sweet tune is like medicine to the heart.
Its rhythm will be just right.
Eyes upon eyes will follow a happy face.

My Boy,
If you prefer the peace sign,
Love will follow.

My Boy, along life's journey you must be humanlike.
Stay away from pride.
Dream of great things for the good of man.
Work that mind of yours to heal a broken heart.
I have seen man and how far he is gone,
A face that begs for a loving hand.

My Boy,
Let us be thankful for a sound mind.
Let us live our lives that others may follow.
Away with ego and allow humility to take its course.

August 7, 2009

AT THE ROCK

At the rock two elders rushing to look at the names of the dead.
Facing the East I stand.
What sorrows have I seen in the eyes of the elders?
My God, the hands of evil let loose upon a nation.
What drove men to feed upon such rage?
What hearts were they fitted with?
Father, in your name I pray for peace.
Let this nation find the will to forgive.
Help your people to mourn their dead.
In their memory grant us the wisdom to love again.

August 7, 2009

DANCE WITH ME

My Boy,
If hatred should find your heart,
Do not allow it to grow.
Let love be your darling.
Love itself shall be your soul mate.

My Boy,
Dance that others may follow.

August 7, 2009

THE SPIRIT OF LOVE

Come, My Boy,
Come, let us find a place to reason.
From your young mind to this old mind,
We shall find a common ground.

My Boy,
When I look at your eyes,
I have seen something good in you.
You possess the spirit to love.
Your charm and personality have attracted many eyes.

My Boy,
For the good of humanity,
Use your God-given gift for the good of man.

My Boy,
If you feed a child upon that which is good,
Such a child will produce that which is good.

My Boy,
Heap no shame upon the suffering man.
Comforting words are good for the soul.
Forget not the hands of the Good Shepherds.

My Boy,
I leave in peace.
Go and do your Father's work.

August 7, 2009

HARD TIMES

My Boy,
These are hard times.
I shall lay blame upon no one.
I came with nothing, and I shall return with nothing.

My Boy,
Why then should I worry?
The great Father is in charge.
I am just a humble servant.
Time will tell about this period.
Man shall live and man shall die.
Let this heart beat until it ceases.

August 7, 2009

FRAMING WORDS

My Boy,
I shall use courage to frame these words.
For the love of humanity I will allow the human spirit to
feed upon comforting words.
Life and its journey are not easy.

My People,
Be strong.
Find that faith and hold on.
Feed upon hope and dream along.
Forget not your knees.
Use them, then cry to a Higher Power.

Power Higher Than I,
You have seen the frustration of your people.
Something needs to be done.
Give unto us a leader that will lead.
Great inspiration, I pray today.
Today I call upon thee.
Send us another Moses.
The rise of hatred is creating havoc upon the society.
Man and his rise to power need to be in check.

August 7, 2009

WHEN I MET YOU

My Boy,
When I met you,
I refused to go into a state of panic.
Love almost pulled my feet from the floor.
I had to control myself.
The voices of the elders reassured my stand.
Deep faith and praying hands lifted my spirit.
Well, then, let me speak of thee while I am alive.
I will use your face to guide my thoughts.

My Boy,
It was meant to be.
You are the poster child for love.
I shall paint a picture of you for the world to see.
Even though young at heart,
Your name is upon the lips of many.

My Boy,
Go and spread that love.

August 8, 2009

WHY DO YOU WRITE ABOUT LOVE?

Why do you write so much about love?
My people, a happy heart feeds upon love.
What is love?
A poet in his moment of peace and tranquility will allow
love to find his soul.
My people, love is that happiness that boosts the spirit.
When there is love,
There will be no room for hatred.
If you pray for love,
Love will come to you.
As I watch the hands of time,
I tell you no lies.
True love comes to me.
My people, with these tears let me send my love.
Do not be afraid to feed upon that which is good.
Today the good God knows my heart.
My people, one love.

August 8, 2009

READ ABOUT THIS MAN

If you find the time to read about this man,
You will feel his godliness.
A man willing to expose his inner feelings,
An in-depth love for humanity,
A touch of spirituality springs from his soul.
A man sets out on a journey preparing for his destiny.

August 8, 2009

THE BIRDS CAME

My Boy,
Birds upon birds came to sing for I and I.
Two cats in waiting.
Oh! What a beautiful morning.
The sun is in its glory.
I and I live to see another day.
Let me be thankful and give praises.

Father, mine eyes have seen the working of your hands.
Nature bound I lift my spirit.
Oh! What a glorious day.

August 8, 2009

GOOD NIGHT MY BOY

Good night my boy.
Good night by boy.
Grandpa is a little bit tired tonight after a hard day's work.
Grandpa will try to get some sleep.
As I pray, sweet sleep I hope to find.

My boy, what I have seen with these eyes took a hold of me.
Man and his troubled mind I cannot escape.
Even though the work must be done,
The weight is more than I.
Blessed Father, you have seen what I have seen.
Let me find the courage to go on.

My Lord, my years I have invested for the good of man.
Help me to rise to the task.
Father, I shall go to sleep now.
Let my dreams be sweet.
When I arise, the East shall be my course.
The eyes of the fallen man I shall seek to find.

August 9, 2009

CONTRIBUTION

My Boy,
If I can make a contribution to mankind,
May the words I put together be it.

My Boy,
I do not have much, but I am willing,
Willing to take a stand against injustice.
Willing to lend a hand to the suffering man.

My Boy,
I have lived a life with others in mind.
I did not allow pride to blind my eyes.
One heart, one voice for the good of man.

My Boy,
I am near my journey now.
Along the way, look for your instructions.
Take them to the heart of man.

August 10, 2009

MY CRAFT

My Boy,
In my craft of cultivating love,
I pray that reapers may find the joy.
A full life and a full love.
Fine gold without love does not bring happiness.
Today I look at man on his final journey.
Tears upon tears fell upon him.
The musicians playing *Nearer My God To Thee*.
I said to myself, "What is man? Time will tell."

My Boy,
Indulge not in reaping the wealth.
Remember your brothers and sisters.
Live and let others live.
Harden not your heart against the fallen man.
Be a student of love.
Rise up to be the best at your game.
This old hand I shall lift up for thee.
Oh, great sun, I shall look beyond thee.

August 10, 2009

LADY IN BLUE

Lady in Blue,
Come to me that I may fix my eyes.
Your jumping lips I shall seek thereof.
For the good of man,
Let us unite to fight for a just cause.
You came, you looked and you learned.
The weary souls are at a loss.
May your dignity lift their spirit.

My Lady,
There must be a reason you came on board.
The good God must have sent you.
I think I shall never see another one like you.
Even though they come and go,
You are the lady of the house.
Rise up and do what you do best.
The fallen man shall rise again.
Come sing with me that I may fine-tune my music.

August 10, 2009

A HEAD WITH WORDS

My Boy,
Today words took over my head.
Great spirits, come to my defense.
With this heart I cannot rest.
The test of summer at its best.
Man crying out for cool water.
Words fighting to get into the pool.
A fool with pen in hand trying to be cool.
The power of words stimulate the mind.
Angry words I do not need.
Sweet dancing words, I shall carry along.
For the love of humanity, may these words be a cooler
to the heart of man.

August 10, 2009

COME, MY LORD

Awake, my spirit.
Awake, my spirit.
The eyes of the suffering man await thee.
My God, westbound I and I shall go.
The heart of the suffering man robbed me of my sleep.
How cold I find sweet sleep when his eyes find my soul?

My Lord, duty and only duty is my cry.
The work must be done.
Who am I not to follow my calling?

Great Protector of man,
You have seen the task ahead of I and I.
A bold spirit I beg of thee.
Father, teach me thy ways that I may be able to do the work.
The return of man I beg of thee.
What sorrows have I seen?
Come, my Lord.
Come to his rescue.

August 10, 2009

BE NEAR ME

My Boy,
When I write for thee,
The words I find are covered with love.
Love and only love,
I shall present to thee.

My Boy,
I cannot leave my love alone.
God must have sent you.

My Boy,
Even though you are so far away,
When my time is near,
Be near me that I can fix mine eyes.

My Boy,
Remember I found my words through a higher source.
Take what is yours.
When this hand is laid to rest,
On this day, at this hour your face I shall carry with me.

My Boy,
One love.

August 10, 2009

LOOKING AT MAN

My God,
When I look at man,
I say to myself, "What can madness do?"
Man not in his right frame of mind feeds upon your heart.

Father, even though fear took a grip on me,
Let me find the courage to give of myself.

Father, with you all things are possible.
Let me see the light that I may be able to do the right thing.
If only I could find the right words.
Man to man I would stand.
Mine eyes would be fixed.
Clearance, my Lord, I would beg of thee.
Here are my hands.
Let me find the fire I need.

August 10, 2009

A CHOICE

My Dear,
Why should I hate when I have a choice to love?
I care not of your earthly gains.
When you are called,
Nothing will be yours.
As for me,
A smiling face will be a blessing.
If I cannot work for the good of man,
Why was I born?
Why should I gain when I could give?

August 11, 2009

GOING HOME

My Love,
I shall not be late for sunset.
I and I shall bid thee farewell.
Now that you are on your way to a better place,
May the angels await thee.
I shall do my best to prepare myself.
I shall set my eyes upon my wings.

My Love,
I did not leave any tears.
Your good deeds I remember.
In your name I shall find words to mark your spot.

My Love,
Go to that place where we shall meet again.

August 11, 2009

A JOURNEY

Awake, my spirit.
Awake, my sprit.
The sun is upon us.
Let me find a place that I can warm myself.
A warm spot is needed for the journey.
Within the mountain, the House of Suffering sits.
What heart will I carry?

Father, I pray for a loving heart.
A cool head I shall need.
Father, if only I could find healing words,
My day would be sweet.

August 12, 2009

KEEPING MY MUSIC

My Boy,
I write because I cannot keep my music.
The heart of man I seek to find.
Sweet music, my boy, is good for the soul.
The lifting of the spirit, I pray.

August 12, 2009

LET ME BE WHO I AM

Let me strive to be who I want to be.
Have I not a brain like the others?
Well, then, let me be who I want to be.

August 12, 2009

I HAVE GIVEN MY LOVE

Oh! Dear, I have given the love out of me.
It's too late now for me to shed tears.
When I find this sleep,
May sweet dreams stay with me.

August 12, 2009

I PRAY FOR YOU

My Boy,
I write because my heart is free from hatred.
A loving heart I shall present to thee.
I pray for your young heart.
While I am around, I shall find words to carry my love.

My Boy,
If you follow a loving path, the pain of hatred will find no room.

My Boy,
Allow history to find your name on the side of good.

August 12, 2009

COME MY LOVE

My Love,
How can I not speak to thee and live?
I have felt the moment of loneliness.
I care not if I run after thee.
Your heels shall find my eyes.
Laughter, my love, will be no match for my ears.
The power of love shall pull me through.

Go, my love, and I will follow.
A loving heart shall seek that which is good.
Come, my love, come to me.

August 12, 2009

BRING ME YOUR HANDS

My Boy,
Bring me your little hands.
How beautiful they are.
Power higher than I blessed these hands for the good of man.

My Boy,
Use your young hands to plant good seeds.
Use your eyes to look for bad weeds.

My Boy,
Bad weeds will choke everything that is good.
Be on the lookout to be swift with your hands.

My Boy,
If I cannot share my learning with you,
It will be of no use to the grave.
Well, then, let me continue to speak.

My Boy,
Be humble to a point that you become humanlike.
Pull from your heart everything that is good.
Let your hands be a symbol for peace.

My Boy,
One love.
Peace be with you.

August 12, 2009

THE ROAD I CHOOSE

My Boy,
The road I choose, the suffering man will not leave.
Day by day, their eyes I find.
Oh! Suffering man, what shall I do?
Even though I am willing and able,
The working of the mind I cannot control.
I shall try to do my best.
Oh! Love, take me to the heart of the suffering man.
Let my hands be willing to serve.
A loving heart I pray to carry.
A man in great need needs some good hands.

My Lord,
Let their pain be my pain,
Their pleasure mine also.
Work upon this heart that I may give of myself.
Human dignity shall be my cry.

August 12, 2009

WHAT PLEASURE

Brown skin, you generate so much pleasure,
That I took time out to write for thee.
I shall choose my words with care.
I beg of you, let your beauty shine.
Your eyes can create magic.
For the good of humanity,
I beg you to take a stand.
You have seen the weary souls.
Use your charm to brighten their spirit.
As for me, I shall keep watch.

My Lady, do not be afraid to use your tongue.
The Great Protector will take you along.
I have seen something good in you.
In what pleasure you brought to the eyes.
Go, my Lady, and do your Father's work.

August 12, 2009

SWEET LOVE

Sweet Love,
Thy lips shall not go to waste.
For the good of man, allow jumping words to find the heart of man.
The good God must have sent you.
Look at the eyes.
Are they not bright?

Sweet Love,
Work those lips.
Reach for the soul.
Bring forth the good from within.
Do not be afraid, Sweet Love.
A higher power is at work.
Work upon your calling,
Then I shall weep no more.

August 12, 2009

BEFORE YOU

Oh! Heavenly Father, as I bow before thee,
The burden of man I take to thee.
What sorrows have I seen?
Man fallen from grace.
What pity, in what shame have I seen?
Father, I come to thee a humble man.
For the good of man, touch this hand,
A hand that I shall use to carve words.
Comforting words I shall put to His lips.
The return of this lost soul, I pray.
Sweet songs I shall sing.
If only I could charm this heart,
My day would be sweet.
Father, in your name I pray.
Let me find a song of victory.

August 12, 2009

YOUR HANDS, MY LORD

Today I am looking at the sun.
My thoughts I shall allow to go beyond.
For the good of man, let me pray.
Blessed Father, on this day I beg of thee.
Come to the aid of the suffering man.
Unknown voices took over his head.
The pain took much from him.
My Lord, your hands I seek.
Let this man return to the fold.
Use him that others may see.

In my head I cannot rest.
The working of the mind I cannot understand.
Oh! Father, only you can touch this man.
Lay your hands upon him that he may be well again.
Give unto him the fire he needs.

August 12, 2009

WHAT RAGE

My Dear,
What rage thou possess.
Such display is not good for the heart.
With time, the wound will be healed.
Find your knees to find that inner peace.
Use your mind to fashion that which is good.

My Dear,
Remember life is short.
Peace and love, My Dear, should be your cry.
Today I come to you with love.
Come to me.
Come to me.
Let us go and do our Father's work.

August 12, 2009

DREAM ON

My God,
Be merciful to this hand,
A hand that I have worked for the good of man.

Blessed Father,
You have seen the hardship of this hand.
Its fingers working to the bones.
Yet I dream on.

August 12, 2009

STRANGE

My Dear,
I shall cast my hands in words.
The working of the mind you shall find.

August 13, 2009

FLIGHT

Leave my, my love.
Let your heels find sparks.
When you run out of gas,
Let me be your reserve tank.

August 13, 2009

FORGIVE ME

My Dear,
Forgive me if I leave your face behind.
In the dead of night,
I shall awake my memory.

August 13, 2009

I STAND BEFORE YOU

My Dear,
I cannot allow the eyes to wonder.
The heart needs something good.
Come to me with thy beauty.
Let this heart find its rhythm.
Today I stand before thee.
Here are my hands.
Come walk with me.
If I have to sing for thee, let it be my dear.

August 14, 2009

FEELINGS

My Dear,
The power of love took a hold of me.
Sweet sleep I will not allow my eyes.
The stars I shall follow.
My thoughts I shall allow to feed upon sweet words.
Oh! Praying hands, forget me not.
Let my life be a mirror to others.
Peace and love I pray.
My people, if your eyes should find me,
Come and let us reason.

August 14, 2009

BY THE MOUNTAIN

My Lord, My Lord,
By the mountain where I stand,
The sun, my Lord, is upon me.
The working of the mind I set upon thee.
The time is right for me.
The winds passing through.
Man and woman building a fountain of love.
Where are the children?
Oh! Yes, what a beautiful morning.
Peace I pray for this hand.
Yes, a nation under the spell of troubled times.

Oh, Lord, hear the cry of this man.
Early I rise to find thee.
My Lord, this morning my spirit turns to thee.
I know not why the burden of man rests upon me.
This heart within me is full.
Peace and prosperity I pray.

Father, I will sit and watch the clouds for thee.
With this hand I lift to thee.
For the good of man, send some help to this land.
A land of plenty, yet the suffering goes on.
Greed, my Lord, showing its ugly face.
Man selling his soul to have his frame with fine gold.
When will it end?

Father, come to our rescue.

August 14, 2009

NO AMOUNT OF TEARS

I moved my lips but could not speak.
What power the eyes generate.
Words I knew, I could not find.
What power do the eyes possess?
Face to face I cannot stand.
No amount of years is good enough.

August 14, 2009

RUNNING AFTER THEE

Sweet Love,
I do not run after thee for fun.
The power of love sets my feet on fire.
Yes, dear, I said fire.
How could I not run when the fire is too hot for me?

My Friends,
What is this?
I moved my lips but could not speak.
How see your laughter sounds.
What pleasure can we share?
What home can we share?
Which dreams can come to light?
What pleasure can daylight bring?

Oh, Sweet Love,
I do not run after thee for fun.
When the harvest is right,
Let me drink from your cup.

August 14, 2009

I COME WITH JUMPING LIPS

My Dear,
How can I move on when my heart is not what it used to be?
How can I walk alone when I need a hand?
What are prayers for?
Deep faith, my dear, will remove all fear.
Have I not gone on my knees?
Death, the stealer of man would find me.
Well then, my dear, I come to you with jumping lips.
Hear my cries.
Lend me your hands.

August 14, 2009

DUTY

Awake, my spirit.
Awake, my spirit.
The voice of the suffering man is calling.
Eastbound here I come.
Blessed Father, you have seen my journey.
Come with me that I may not be afraid.

August 15, 2009

FIGHTING WORDS

I write to free my spirit from choking words.
Words I knew not came with a fighting spirit.
For the good of man, this hand must play its path.

August 15, 2009

WHAT ABOUT LOVE?

Love, what about love?
My people, it's that inner feeling,
A joyful heart, my people, is good for the soul.
A life lived without love is not worthy.
Every man that trod upon this land should leave this place
a better place.

August 15, 2009

COME BEFORE IT'S TOO LATE

My Child,
Come to me.
Come to me before it's too late.
There is no remembrance from the grave.
Oh! Child of the Most High,
Forget not your Father's teachings.

August 15, 2009

THE WORKING OF A POET

A poet on his journey will find time,
Time to work at his craft.
A poet will set his eyes upon his wings.
No darkness will beat him down.
A poet reaching for the heavens will call upon his God.
Then prepare the food for the harvest.

August 15, 2009

THE EYES OF DEATH

The eyes of death, cold and brutal, I cannot stand.
Yet I stand at attention.

August 15, 2009

GAIN YOUR WINGS

No, I am not Doctor Love.
I am just a simple man trying to get by.
If I practice good deeds,
All honor be upon my parents.
Boy, they are poor.
Never turn your back upon them.
With those words I built upon them.
The lover for humanity took a hold on me.
The suffering of man feeds upon this heart.
Dry lips I cannot leave.
Father, let me find the will to do what I love to do.
Crying out loud shall be my theme.
The work must be done.
Do not weep, Good Shepherds.
Gain your wings and go to a better place.

August 15, 2009

THE TRUTH

My People,
Brace with me to call upon the hands of justice.
Let fairness be upon your hand.
Let not the blood of a brother be upon our hands.
Look at your maker, then look at man with a sound mind
and make your choice.
In the name of justice,
Release your heart from the pain.
As for me,
I will allow my conscience to set me free.
I cam with nothing, and I shall return with nothing.

August 15, 2009

AWAIT MY SONG

Sweet Love,
Await my song.
Strong lips will allow a high pitch.
Let your ears be mine.
Hide not your eyes from mine.
What secret passion I find.
Listen to my voice,
Then ride that rhythm.
Let love be love.

August 14, 2009

MAN AND BOY

My Boy,
On meeting you, you gave me the joy to live again.
Where my youth had gone, it returned again.
Even though many years had passed,
With due modesty I shall allow my youthful spirit to play.
With your sweet voice singing, "Play, Grandpa. Play, Grandpa.
Nice Grandpa. Nice Grandpa,"
My feet I shall use to excite your curious mind.
In the history of true love we shall allow the presence of these eyes.
The meeting of the minds.
In memory of this day.
The praying hands.
The joyous hearts.
May the Father of all fathers seal and sign our love.
Man and boy finding love at first sight.

My Boy,
Love is a good thing.

August 21, 2009

MY BOY NUMBER TWO

My Boy Number Two,
As I await your arrival, let me pray.

Blessed Father,
Let mother and child be safe.

My Boy,
From the dark I pray that you will see the light.
I might not be there to hear your first cry, but I was there
for your mother.

My Boy,
I wish you a safe journey.
Oh! Love, take me where my heart belongs.
To you, my boy, I send my love.

My Boy,
Remember now that one this day I trained my thoughts to
find thee.
No mountain, no valley shall dampen my spirit.
With the blessing of the Most High, we shall meet—Grandpa
and Grandson.

August 21, 2009

HELP ME

Blessed Father,
As I lift my heart to thee,
Help me to find good thoughts.
Teach me that I may prepare myself.
For the love of humanity I come to thee.
Peace and love I pray.
Let man find the will to love again.

August 29, 2009

I ASK FOR LOVE

I ask for love,
That I may find light feet.
Give me the light that I may come after thee.
Make me a lover of thee,
That I may watch over thee.
Give me such courage that I weep with joy.

September 2, 2009

WORDS OF INSPIRATION

Father, from the rock I cry to thee.
The sun I will not leave.
For the good of man, I come to thee.
Words of inspiration I beg of thee.
Men of old found thy ears.
Today I alone look beyond the sun to find thee.
The plight of man rests upon me.
What madness I have seen in man.

Father, what shall I do?
I cannot turn back now.
My years I have dedicated to a just cause.
Now that my mind is fresh,
Fill me up that I may give of myself.
Help me to shake my hands with a good heart.

September 3, 2009

A HAPPY FACE

My Dear,
Be humble and walk that good walk.
For the uplifting of man,
Let your beauty shine.
Use your lips to move comforting words.
Hide not your eyes from the suffering man.
Leave not his sadness untouched.
A happy face will attract his spirit.

September 3, 2009

JUSTICE

Oh! Weeping man,
I care not if the grave awaits what is left.
Justice and only justice shall be our cry.
The pain must take its course.
Stand up face justice like a real man.

September 4, 2009

81

TWO BOYS

My Boy, Tristan, I shall report to you from my dwelling.
Let me speak.
Remember you are not alone now.
Your little brother should be your eyes.
Love, my boy, should be upon your lips.

Let me pray.
Blessed Father, at this hour, here I am.
Remember these two boys.
May their years be many.
For the good of man,
Let them find the path of the Good Shepherds.

As for me, I shall keep watch.
As I follow the hands of time,
So shall I follow their growth.

My God, at this moment I have reached for my soul.
Have mercy upon these two boys.
Even though they are too young to understand,
Let peace and love be with them.

September 4, 2009

HOW SWEET

How sweet it was hearing that sweet voice,
A voice that touches the heart,
A heart that is silent in love.
Since then, these ears stand at alert.
My dear, the mover of souls, I commend you.
My thoughts enjoy a sudden burst of laughter.
Moving feet I cannot control.
Sweeter than honey they chanted.
My dear, help me to be still.
I thank thee for lending me your sweet voice.
Good God, in Your name let me pray.
Let me find the courage to stand and face the music.
Let happiness be a cooler to this heart.
Sweeter than honey, lift up your voice again.

September 4, 2009

MY PEOPLE

My Dear,
I shall write for those who love me.
I shall write for those who hate me.
The words I find are not mine.
I have used this heart to find the true God.
Who am I to feed upon hatred,
When I pray to feed upon that which is good?
I will not allow my soul to be tainted.
My mind is set upon a higher calling.

My Brothers and Sisters,
If you find my hands,
Do not be afraid to walk with me.
I have gone on my knees to clear my path.
The words I find are before your very eyes.
One love, may peace be with you.

September 4, 2009

HOW SWEET IT WAS

My Boy,
How sweet it was, seeing you again.
Young at heart and bold as a lion.
The priest was no match for you.
A job to be done and you were prepared.
In view of many eyes,
The holy water brought joy to the heart.

My Boy,
What memory do I hold?
A man is never too old to learn,
The right spot at the right time.
The eyes will fatten the spirit.

My Boy,
I moved my lips but could not sing.
What pleasing scene have I witnessed?
A strange city but you let me feel welcome.

My Boy,
At 3:00 AM, I pledge to honor thee.
What pride do I hold?
From this hand may true love come to thee.
Let me pray.
Blessed Father, forget not our eyes.

September 5, 2009

MY FATHER

My Dear Father,
Let me find a way to follow my dreams.
For the love of humanity,
My mind cannot rest.
Great things I dream of.
The eyes of the suffering man will not leave.

Father,
If I am pointing in the right direction,
Let me find the courage to press on.

September 5, 2009

IN LOVE

My Dear,
In love I shall prepare to lay down my life.
If I cannot stand as a man,
What purpose do I serve?
Well, then, let my manhood speak for me.
Step by step I shall watch over thee.
No evil hands will I allow in sight.
Duty, my dear, and only duty shall be my cry.
The work must be done.
Be still my soul.
Let my hand do the talking.

September 5, 2009

FORGIVE ME

My Dear,
Forgive me because my love comes so bold.
Love itself shall be my music.
How can I hide when I am driven by fire?

My Dear,
Cool water I seek.

My Dear,
If you find my poor mind in need,
Rise up and be my love.
I love thee more than the eyes I have seen.
Forgive me, my dear, if my love comes so bold.

September 8, 2009

A FACE

My Boy,
What sweetness thy face brings.
A loving heart I can feel.
Let us unite for the good of man.
In secret I shall allow my heart to be lifted up.

My Boy,
Go to the roots of your ancestors.
Look at their hands.
For the love of humanity they lend a helping hand.
As for me, my hands will be among the praying hands.
I shall send my soul with words.

My Boy,
Feed upon the words,
Then go to the heart of man.
Let not my years be wasted.

My Boy,
If you follow my footsteps,
Your eyes shall find your name going to the House of God.

September 9, 2009

THE LIFTING OF THE SPIRIT

Oh! Sweeter than honey, come to me, come.
Let us reason.
For the good of man, let your beauty shine.
Look, my dear, the eyes of the suffering man are upon you.
What pity have I seen.
My dear, harden not your heart.
We are all God's children.
My dear, if I find comforting words, will you roll them for me?
The lifting of the spirit is a must.

September 9, 2009

BEFORE MY SPIRIT

My Boys,
Before my spirit returns to the Most High,
I shall look upon the sun and dream along.

My Boys,
Comfort me with nothing but love.
As I look beyond the sun,
I pray to find the ears of the Most High.

Boys,
This old man shall enter your names.
Long life, my boys, I pray.
The love for humanity.
I expect great things from you both.

September 10, 2009

LABOR

My Dear,
I will labor for thy love.
Day by day I shall come to thee.

My Dear,
There is no joy without love.
I shall come to thee.
What are eyes for?
I will not be afraid of the false lips.
Raw eyes I care not.
You and only you I shall serve.
Have I not a mind of my own?
Then I will allow no man to think for me.

September 10, 2009

THOSE SWEET LIPS

My Dear,
Those sweet lips that moved the hearts of men now lay dead to the eyes.
The earth will hide what is left.
Flowers will bloom and drop their seeds upon her.
Birds will take what is theirs.
No more glitter, no more gold.
All the fame could not keep her stay.
Her little frame is now lined with dirt.
The children came playing upon her.
Old eyes with head bowed confront her spot.
What evil hands took her from us so soon.
True God, in your name we pray for justice.

September 10, 2009

PLANT YOUR SEEDS

My Boys,
I shall leave my love alone.
Give unto me no tears.
If I teach you well,
Let my name be upon your lips.
Seek and find the words.

My Boys,
Feed upon the words.
For the love of humanity,
I beg of you boys to follow the path of the Good Shepherds.
Seek the face of the Most High.
Pray to find wisdom.
Then plant your seeds.

September 11, 2009

THE MIND OF THE OLD MAN

My Dear Boy, Tanner,
I shall use this old mind to speak.
Soon I shall leave my words for you to feed upon.

My Boy,
I shall be careful of my selections.
I shall beg of you.
For the good of man,
Put oil in the lamp that the fire keeps burning.

My Boy,
You need the light that you may follow.

My Boy,
Find the ears of the elders.
Pull from the tree of wisdom.
Set your eyes upon the prize.
Duty and only duty should be your cry.

My Boy,
Forget not your roots.
Your ancestors have laid the foundation.
Go now, my Boy, and let us be proud.

September 11, 2009

THE YOUNG AT HEART

To the young at heart,
My friends heap no shame upon the elders.
You know not their journey.
Use your young mind to fashion comforting words.
Remember today for me,
Tomorrow for you.
Live and let others live.
As for me, I am blessed with many years.
My friends, do good and good will follow you.
Boast not of your youthfulness.
I have seen the hearse taking the young and the old along.

My friends, let your work speak for you.
Seek and find the path of the Good Shepherds.
A good name is better than fine gold.
My friends, for the love of humanity,
Today I call upon you.
Turn not your eyes upon the common man.
Reach within your soul and do that which is good.

September 11, 2009

MY DEAR BOY TANNER

My Dear Boy Tanner,
This is your Grandpa.
I shall allow my imagination to find thee.
Feed on, my dear boy.
I shall await your eyes.

Blessed Father,
At this hour, I come to thee.
Bless this boy that he may strive for the good of man.
Let me live that we may bless our eyes.

My Father,
Fine gold have I now.
Let me find sweet words for his tongue.

My Boy,
When the time is right,
Go into the world and do that which is good.
Today I have gone deep within my soul.
I shall pour out my heart for you to see.
This hand, my boy, I shall ask of you to carry.

My Boy,
Do not be ashamed.
I have washed it.
As I follow the hands of time,
Feed on, my dear boy.

September 11, 2009

I PRAY FOR THIS DAY

My Boy,
I sing to you because of my love.

My Boy,
With a happy heart I shall play a sweet tune.
Doing what is right shall heal all wounds.
God must have sent you in a time of great sorrow.
What joy thy little face brings.
The healing of the soul shall feed upon thee.

Great God,
In your name I pray for peace.
I pray for the meeting of the minds.
I pray for unity.
I pray for this day.
Mine eyes have seen this child.
Let the eyes of the proud take notes.
Awaken my spirit.
Awaken my spirit.
Let us go and spread the good news.
Man and boy sealing their love.

My Boy, I shall go now.
The mountain awaits I and I.

September 11, 2009

WHAT SWEETNESS

My Dear,
What sweetness thy presence brings.
God must have sent you.
Look at those eyes.
What joy have I seen?

My Dear,
Leave us not.
Work with me, my dear.
Work and gain your wings.
They are all God's children.
I cannot leave now.
I am too far gone.
My years I have dedicated to fight for a just cause.
Let us unit and do our best.

September 12, 2009

PEACE

My Boy,
While I pray, the hands of God I shall seek for thee.
May your young heart feed upon that which is good.
Alone I stand before the Great One.
Great blessings I shall be for thee.
On the subject of humanity,
I pray that you will work to leave this world a better place.
Courage, my dear boy, you shall muster.
Live and let others live.
Line not your heart with fine gold.
Remember the suffering man.
If he is hungry, feed him.
Turn not your head from the weeping man.

My Boy,
Along life's journey, be humanlike.
Bring out the beauty from within.
Let your music play for the heart of man.
Today I took from my soul that which is good.
May you find the words comforting to your heart.

My Boy,
I come with peace and I shall leave with peace.

September 12, 2009

FERTILE GROUND

My Boy,
Today I am on the grounds of higher learning.
I pray that you will find my hands.
The working of the mind should be for the good of man.

My Boy,
Remember the common man.
Be willing to teach him what is right from what is wrong.

My Boy,
The work must be done.
Today I shall call upon you to remember this day.
The rain, my boy, shall be my witness.

September 12, 2009

AN ACTIVE MIND

My Boy,
When you do find an active mind,
Find the time to stimulate it.
I do wish you would listen to this old man.
Wisdom, my boy, will not come overnight.
Feed your young mind upon that which is good.
Today I await the sun.
Dark clouds blinded my eyes.
Patience, my boy, I will allow to take its course.

My Boy,
In your quest for knowledge,
It takes time.

My Boy,
A foolish man has no time to improve upon his status.

My Boy,
Invest everything in your youth.
After awhile you will get the return.
A wise man is hard to find.

My Boy,
I will always remember you in prayer.
At this hour I am with the mountain.
My thoughts I have captured for thee.
Go now and let me be proud.

September 12, 2009

DRINK, MY DEAR

Drink, my dear.
Drink and cool thy thirst.
Moisten thy lips with cool water.
Cracked lips will be of no use.
Come, my dear.
Let us go to the fountain.
Look, my dear.
Birds and all doing what is right.

September 15, 2009

MY BOY, THE SECOND

My Boy Tanner,
As I await sweet sleep,
Your name I shall lift up to the Most High.
As I pray,

Blessed Father,
At this hour, I beg of thee.
Remember this little boy.
May he be blessed with many years.
Soften his heart for the good of man.
Father, help him to live by the words.

By Boy,
Do not allow pride to destroy your steps.
If you see a man fall,
Turn not your head.
Let your hands work for you.
Even though young at heart,
Muster the courage to do that which is good.

My Boy,
Sleep will not come.
The working of the mind is set upon thee.
May this hand find favor with you.

September 16, 2009

IN THESE TROUBLED TIMES

My Dear,
In these troubled time,
Only God knows where we are going.
The fall of a nation is in full view.
Where have the good people gone?
A few with thick lips line their hearts with greed.
The rich getting richer and the poor getting poorer.

My God,
Have you not seen the plight of your people?
Where are the Good Shepherds?
How long, my Lord, shall the few prosper?
Where is justice?
Where is love?
How long, my Lord, shall this hardship be upon your people?

Today I come to you on bending knees.
Your people crying out to thee.
Father, have mercy upon us.
Turn things around that we may sing again.
The cries of the poor are all over the land.
This is a land of plenty,
Yet men are begging for bread.

September 17, 2009

AN EVIL MIND

An evil mind will breed evil.
Well, then, my friends,
Train your minds to feed upon love.
Are we not our children's keepers?
If you feed a child upon that which is good,
Such a child will produce that which is good.

My friends,
Life is short.
Allow your stay to be pleasing.
Rise up, my friends.
Rise up to let this world be a better place.
Let history be kind to you.

September 18, 2009

A DREAM

My Boy,
What in the world am I doing at the mountain?
Is it because of the beauty of nature,
Or is it for the good of man?

My Boy,
I shall pause for a moment.
The love for humanity I cannot hide.
Well, then,
Allow me to form my thoughts.
Let me pray.

Blessed Father,
At this moment I shall look beyond the sun.
Father, let my work speak for me.

My Boy,
I shall push myself to be the best I can.
As for you, I wish thee well.
May the good God guide and protect you.

My Boy,
For your young mind,
I shall pray to find words that will enrich your growth.
You will be my young hands.

My Boy,
The work must be done.
The world needs some good hands.
Dream on, my boy, for the good of man.

Oh, Holy One,
In your hands I commit this boy.
Let him rise up for the good of man.

September 18, 2009

THOSE EYES

My Dear,
When I look into your eyes,
What inner peace I have seen.
The moving of the lips pulls my spirit.
Come, my dear.
Let us work for the good of man.
You have seen the sorrows I have seen.
I beg of you, use your beauty for uplifting the spirit.

My Dear,
The good God must have sent you.
Keep your head up.
Let your light shine.
Day by day, I shall pray for thee.

My Dear,
Do not be afraid.
A higher power is upon thee.
Your steps shall be guarded.

My Dear,
Come walk with me.
The work must be done.

September 19, 2009

DEATH

My Dear Boy,
An old man is not less than a young man.
Death can come at any time.

September 19, 2009

AWAY IN THE SUNSET

Away in the sunset,
The Father giveth and the Father taketh.
On this day, our deal love will be going home.
Home, sweet home, my dear.
May the angels await thee.
Heaven-bound I pray.
Blessed Father, you have seen our eyes.
The sadness of our hearts cries for thee.
Have mercy upon us.
The return of our loved one is in your hands.
Thy Lord, sweet music from they servants.
Hands finding thy ears.
Lift up our spirits that we may praise thee.
Let our hearts find comfort in thee.
Take away the sadness that we may strive to do our best.
Our dearly beloved has done her best.
May her rest be sweet.

September 20, 2009

WHAT HAVE I SEEN

My Dear,
What have I seen?
Pure beauty, I hope.
Even though mine eyes fade,
What I have seen, I have seen.

My Dear,
My heart is full.
Let me sit before I fall.
Mine eyes have seen what I have seen.

September 20, 2009

DREAMS

My Boy,
From the dark I rise.
Sweet dreams will never leave.
Your face I have seen,
Yet I could not speak.
The working of the mind will not cease.
Now I shall go to the mountain and rest.
To the East I shall await the sun.
Then I shall ponder over my dreams.

My Boy,
You were music to me.
The arrival of little birds with their sweet songs stimulates an
old memory.

My Boy,
I shall fear no more.
The sun is upon me.
I shall go now.
Then await the night to come again.

September 20, 2009

IF I CANNOT LOVE

My Boy,
If I cannot love thee,
Why should I live?
What more principle would I hold?
What heart would I carry?

My Boy,
Blessed are the peacemakers.
You came to this land for a purpose.
You allowed me to find a new heart.
The hope and dreams of a better world,
Human misery cannot leave untouched.

My Boy,
I shall pray for a new spirit.
I beg of thee, let true love be your tool.

My Boy,
If I did good with this hand,
The love for humanity drove me to preach.
Harden not your heart for the good of man.
True love, my Boy, will soften your heart.
Study the words,
Then go on your journey.
If you feel my mind,
Remember this day as I watch the hands of time.

September 20, 2009

TAKE ME

My Lord, My Lord,
Take me to the House of the Suffering Man.
There awaits my hands.
Father, if fright takes hold of me,
Walk with me.
The work must be done.
Wondering eyes need your hands.

Father, for the good of man,
Today I call upon thee.
Spur me that I may gallop with good strapped to my back.

Father, take me while I am in my prime.
When I remember the wondering spirits,
A part of me weeps.
Man and his troubled mind took a hold of me.
What shall I do?

Father, I am nothing without you.
Let me find the courage to do that which is good.
Today I come before you a humble man,
A man from a far away land lifting up the burden of man,
My hands I present to thee.
Oh! Take me that I may do the job.

September 21, 2009

A MAN OF CONSCIENCE

Come, my dear, I shall eat with you.
Let me offer the peace sign.
May our thoughts be sweet.
Blessed Father, at this hour may your blessing be upon us.
My dear, for the good of man, I pray for your hands.
My dear, listen to a song of praise in the air.
Let us rise up for the good of man.
Feed on, my dear, that you may become strong.
The suffering man awaits thy hands.
My dear, forget not that we are brothers and sisters.
We are all God's children.
The fall of one should not leave our sight.
My dear, you are blessed.
Come fort, my dear, and lend a helping hand.
The rise of the fallen man, I pray.
My dear, remember today for me, tomorrow for you.

September 21, 2009

PEACE AND PROSPERITY

Blessed Father,
On this day I come before thee.
The sun and moving clouds I shall follow.
Peace and love, I pray.

Father,
In this time of great need,
Forget not your children.
The tears of a nation are before thee.
Hardship is driving man mad.

My Lord,
How long, how long shall sinner man moan?
The working of your hands, we shall await.
Let peace and prosperity return to this land.

September 22, 2009

COME, MY DEAR

Come, My Dear,
Listen what sweet music I find for thee.
Let your heart feed upon the words.
Today is a day of rejoicing.
The Lord giveth one fine boy.
Let us give praise to the Most High.

Blessed Father,
May this child rise up for the good of man.
Oh! Young soul, as I pray,
May the good Lord watch over thee.
As the sun penetrates your young body,
May your young heart feed upon that which is good.

My Boy,
Your young mind I shall take to the power higher than I.

Blessed Father, with this old mind I come to thee.
Forget not this boy.
Help him to follow the path of the Good Shepherds.

My Dear,
The shaping of this young soul I shall give of myself.
Power higher than I,
Let me find the courage.

My Boy,
Now that I am at the feet of the Most High,
I beg for your hands.
Come let us go and do the Father's work.

My Boy,
The work must be done.

September 22, 2009

JUSTICE

Black or White, justice is justice.
Give unto a man fairness.
Let every man search his heart,
Then rise before his God.

My Brothers,
The grave will not stipulate who is who.
Live a life that others may follow.
Between the ups and downs along life's journey,
Dream on, my brothers.
Be fair and loving.
Life is short.
Stand up for justice.

September 22, 2009

THE BOUNDARIES OF LOVE

My Boy,
I shall confine myself with the boundaries of love.
Your young heart I shall find food for its growth.

My Boy,
A loving family will breed loving children.
Children will be the men and women for the future.

Father of all love,
Teach me thy way.
Help me to find the heart of the children.
Peace and love I shall take with me.

September 22, 2009

PRAISE FOR THE SINGING BOY

Praise for the singing boy.
My boy, how could I not praise thee?
You came with love and you give love.
From your young mind I cannot tell, but before the eyes of the
elders, you find that sweet tune.
Play Grandpa, play Grandpa.
Nice Grandpa, nice Grandpa.
Your hands were mine and mine yours.
Blood to blood finding a common ground.

My boy, your eyes I will always take with me.
Your spirit came with so much fire that I am a new man.
My boy, let us unite for the good of man.
Today I am with the mountain.
Little birds come with such sweet melodies that I am forced to write.
Sweet music is a comfort to the heart.
My boy, as I meditate upon the words, I shall pray for your guidance.
My boy, long life I wish thee.
Whatever it takes, remember the common man.
Let not pride color your eyes.
Go now, my boy, and share that love.

September 22, 2009

A LONG ROAD

My Boy,
It's a long road to where I reach.
I shall shape my destiny to fit the face of man.
The desire of my heart I shall feed with loving words.
The love for humanity I will allow to lift my spirit.
Now that I am in my prime,
The time has come for I and I.
Oh! Destiny may find me pleasing.
Dignity, my boy, I shall allow to drive me along.

My Boy,
When the time is right,
Forget not to look at my journey.
Today as I stop to pause for a moment,
Dreams upon dreams I have to follow.
Dedication and hard work I have to endure.
Why am I taken out of my heart?
The love for humanity pulls my spirit.

My Boy,
When I leave this land,
Do not be afraid to lift your voice.
Go to the heart of the children,
Then feed them upon that which is good.

September 24, 2009

HATRED

My Dear,
I have seen the hatred upon the lips of many.
Their eyes full with fire.
Their hearts jumping like frogs.
When will man learn that his days are numbered?

Father,
You have seen their lips like maggots among the dead.
How long, my Lord, shall those lips move?

Father,
You have seen the eyes of your servants.
Fright took a hold of them.
As I pray, clearance I beg of thee.
The work must be done.

September 24, 2009

ENVY NOT

My People,
Envy not the man that prospers.
You know not his suffering or his wicked ways.
We are all God's children.
The rich and the poor will return to the earth.
Let us be thankful for what we possess.

My People,
A good life should be your choice.
Live and let others live.
Every man will account for his hands.

September 24, 2009

THE FACE OF THE SUN

My Boy,
I shall not be moved.
The face of the sun I shall await.
Oh! What a beautiful morning.
Nature, my boy, is in its full glory.
The clouds clear as crystal.
Man and dog walking along.
Peace and only peace I feel.
Yes, my boy, the sun is showing its face.
What beauty the sky beholds.
Oh! Great sun, the warmer of man,
Mine eyes have seen creation at work.
I, the lonely poet, shall look beyond thy face.

Oh! Great God,
On this beautiful morning I come to thee.
The eyes of the suffering man await some good hands.
Blessed Father, in your name I pray to find comforting words.
Sad eyes I cannot forget.
Today, today I call upon thee.
Send me the fire I need.
The return of man, I pray.

September 26, 2009

THE BEATING OF THE HEART

What sweetness stems from my lips.
Oh! Take me. Oh! Take me to your place.
Let me be upon thee,
That your heart beats for me.
Then and there I shall weep no more.

September 27, 2009

FROM THE HEART

My Dear,
I shall speak to thee from the heart.
On the suffering of man,
What pity I have seen.
A troubled soul crying out for help.
If I had not trained this heart,
I would set fire to my feet.

My Dear,
I cannot leave now.
My hands I will put to use.
Come, my dear, help me to lift his spirit.
Take his frame from the dirt.
Wash him that he may be clean again.

My Dear,
One good deed is better than none.

September 27, 2009

HOLD ON

Come, my dear, let me wipe your tears.
I have seen your pain.
What sorrows find thee?
A true friend will never turn his back.
My dear, hold on.
The dark will find the light.
Great faith, my dear, shall pull you through.
Today I shall be your cane.
Lean on me.
Step by step we shall go forth.
What are friends for?

September 27, 2009

TIME IS SHORT

My Dear,
When I pull from this heart bad weeds I do not need,
The working of the mind I cannot waste.
Time is short and the work must be done.
The uplifting of man I stand accused.
If history should find this man,
May the children read along.

September 27, 2009

MY DEAR BOY TANNER

My Dear Boy Tanner,
What can Grandpa give you?
Poor as I am, I pray hand in hand.
Let the gift of love be with us.

My Boy,
What can these old hands teach thee?
Each soul finds its own rhythm.
God has a purpose for each of us.

My Boy,
Mark your steps with good deeds.
Carry that sweetness in life to share with others.
Do not allow pride to cover your eyes.
Live a life that others may follow.
Boast not of thy youth.
Be kind to your elders.
Let your energy be their light.

My Boy,
Work to gain your wings.

My Boy,
If I teach thee well,
Go into the world and let me be proud.
Remember you are my blood.
Feel the spirits of your ancestry.
Keep the light burning that others may see.

September 29, 2009

MY HANDS

My Boy,
If I set an example for you to follow,
I have taken time out to prepare my hands.
For many years I have taken notes.
I shall share with you some of the things that rest upon my heart.
Give me love and I shall sing like a bird.

Be of good courage.
Use your gift of youthfulness to serve mankind.
Let your light shine for the eyes of man.
Bring out the music from within.

My Boy,
I am just a traveling man,
But I choose to clear my path.
Great things I pray for thee.
May you use your hands for the good of man.
I pray that you find that courage to go on your journey.
Open your eyes and look for the suffering man.
Listen to your heart and do that which is good.
May you remember my hands upon this day.

September 29, 2009

MY BOYS

Come, my boys, let the three of us reason.
Allow the old head to speak.
The soul of humanity we shall look at.
Where are all the good people?
What hatred have I seen?
Life becomes a joke.
How can man be restored?

My boys, let us seek the teaching of the true God.
Let man return to the bread of life.
Without peace and love,
The heart will have no way to turn.
My boys, go and spread the words.
Peace and love, my brothers and sisters.

My boys, are you willing to allow dignity to be your guide?
Well, then, rise up and go to the heart of man.
My boys, with full courage I pray.

October 1, 2009

STRONG LOVE

My Boy,
You came with all I need.
Strong love, my dear boy.
An old heart feeding upon that which is good.
A song of love that made me whole.
Praise God for your sweet voice.
Play, Grandpa. Play, Grandpa.
Nice Grandpa. Nice Grandpa.

Blessed Father,
You have seen this young soul.
A boy finding the will to love.
Who could it be, my Lord, but thee?

Father,
Help me to use this mind to capture the moment.
For the good of man,
May I find comforting words to lift the spirit.

Blessed Father,
With our portion of love,
Let us unite for the soul of humanity.

Father,
As I pray,
May this boy grow in the grace of knowledge.

October 1, 2009

GRANDPA SPEAKING

My Boy,
Keep yourself from hatred.
Life is too short for evil thoughts.
True love, my boy, will bring happiness.
True love will bring peace.

My Boy,
Leave this world a better place.

My Boy,
Find that courage to do the Father's work.
You came to this land for a purpose.
Let no man take away your heart's desire.
When the burden of your heart is too heavy,
Use your knees to call upon a Higher Power.

My Boy,
Allow your dignity to pull the eyes of others.

My Boy,
It is my feeling I turn into words.
Rise up and be humanlike.

October 4, 2009

BETTER THAN FINE GOLD

My Boy,
This Grandpa has a mind of his own.
I shall use it for your growth.
Even though young at heart,
It is my duty to guide you along life's journey.

My Boy,
I have lived for many years.
Let me give thanks to the Most High.
Today I took time out to speak to you.
Let me begin on meeting you.
I have seen something good in you.

My Boy,
Your love will be your weapon.
I beg of you,
Use your gift for the good of man.
A good deed, my boy, is better than fine gold.

October 5, 2009

INSPIRATION

My Boy,
When God needs peace,
The working of His hands will be upon the heart.
From your young mind you came with the words.
Who am I not to love thee?
Your sweet voice will never leave.
Your face I cannot escape.
Your love caught the eyes of many.

My Boy,
You are blessed.
The angels must be upon you.
Never have I seen such blooming love.

My Boy,
Great inspiration I draw from you.
All the heart needs is love.
When love finds the heart of a man,
His mind will be clear.
For the good of man,
He will form his thoughts upon that which is good.
When God is in the picture,
A child will teach the elders.

My Boy,
I have seen something good in you.
Let me pray.

Blessed Father,
At this hour, here are my hands.
Remember this boy.
Let him rise up for the good of man.
Give unto him the food he needs.
Let him find his purpose in life.

My Boy,
As I await the sun,
May you find my hands.

October 5, 2009

MY LITTLE HANDS

Oh! Love, take me to my little hands.
Lift me from the mountain that I may choose my path.
Eyes of mine leave me not.
Let us unite for the good of man.
Awake, my spirit.
The power of love finds my bones.
The voice of the children calling I and I.
No distance, no journey shall stand in my way.
Love will clear all hurdles.

October 5, 2009

FINGERING MY THOUGHTS

My Boy,
Today I face the sun to finger my thoughts.
I shall try to reach beyond to find a higher source.
Words, my boy, I shall try to find.
If I could only find the words for the tongue of man,
My morning would be sweet.
Let me humble myself and await my findings.

Oh, Heavenly Father,
For the good of man, the work must be done.
The burden of man is too much for the eyes.

Father,
What shall I do?
If I could only find comforting words,
The moving of my lips would be in full force.

My Boy,
I will use my knees to find what I need.
Let me brace myself to face the sun.
At this crucial moment,
I cannot leave.
The work must be done.
The working of the mind I shall allow to function.
Great dreams, my boy, I shall follow.
The lifting of the spirit I pray.

October 5, 2009

THE SHAPING OF THE MINDS

My Boys,
I shall be true to my calling.
Sweet dreams I cannot forget.
The light and only the light I shall bring.
Peace and love, my boys, I pray to be our food.

Blessed Father,
Help me to be true to my calling.
Of those in need of love,
Father, let these boys find the will to love.
With this old hand,
The shaping of the minds I pray.

October 5, 2009

A WISH

I pray that these boys and I walk hand in hand.
For the love of humanity, may their young minds feed upon that
which is good.
My boys, we need to leave this place a better place.
I cannot harden my heart against the suffering man.
My boys, if I cannot share the love I hold, why should the sun be
kind to me?
Today I use the sun to warm my spirit.
With a happy heart I shall take a look at dancing trees.
Boys, close not your eyes upon the human suffering.
If you can bring a little joy to one soul, I beg you to go for it.
My boys, if you find this heart to be a loving one, take it to the eyes
of the children.

October 5, 2009

SING YOUR SONG

My Boy,
Sing your song and allow others to find its rhythm.
Play, Grandpa. Play, Grandpa.
Nice Grandpa. Nice Grandpa.
Let the meeting of the minds feed upon that which is good.

Father of all Fathers,
What sweet melodies do I feed upon?
The young at heart in full bloom.
Sing on, my boy.
Let the weary souls be kind to thee.
You came with the blessing of the Most High.
Rise up, my boy, and let your voice be heard.
Let the wandering eyes be still.

My Boy,
Work that rhythm for the soul of man.
Let the goodness of your heart follow the path of the Good Shepherds.

My Boy,
Use your young mind for the good of man.
May the spirits of the Most High find favor with you.

My Boy,
For the good of man,
Let your voice be heard.
Fine-tune that song and let its rhythm flow.

October 6, 2009

HELP

My Boy,
The little child shall lead.
The purity of the young heart shall find peace.
No man shall stand in the path of God's children.

My Boy,
Let us unite our hearts.
Your tender love lifted my spirit.
As I pray, great God, through your spirit,
Speak to the soul of this boy.
Let him find the courage to charm the heart of man.

I have seen the goodness of his heart.
Let me find sweet words for his tongue.
This boy came with love.
How could I not love him in return?

Father,
With a clean heart,
Help me to shape his path.

October 10, 2009

I CANNOT PREDICT THE FUTURE

My Boys,
At this moment I shall use my mind to share my thoughts.
I cannot predict the future,
But I wish you both God's blessing.
On the subject of peace,
When will men find the will to love?
What hatred breeds among men?

Boys,
Pray for a loving heart.
Use your minds to coin loving words.
Find that courage to stand up for justice.
Pray for divine guidance.
I, the holder of the pen, will pray along.

Boys,
I cannot turn back now.
I have invested my years for the good of man.
Who am I not to share the legacy?
My father and his father have laid the foundation.

Boys,
Help me to build upon it.
Now that I have been beaten down by years of service,
I now call upon the both of you.
Take the lead and let me be proud.

October 10, 2009

I STAND

Power Higher than I,
Here I am.
For the love of humanity I stand.
Let the working of the mind produce that which is good.

October 10, 2009

GREAT STRIDES

In my great strides of happiness,
The eyes of a boy I shall follow.
My boy, go to school and feed upon the words.
Use your young mind for the good of man.
My boy, where there is darkness,
Pray to see the light.
Take the light to the eyes of the common man.

As for me,
The sun I shall await.
I shall allow faith to dictate my path.
The purging of the soul I shall allow to take place.
For the love of humanity,
I pray for human dignity,
The lifting of the spirits.
Let me call upon a higher power.

Power higher than I,
For the good of man,
I pray for peace and love.
Where there is hatred,
Let love find its course.
My boy, dream on for a better world.

October 11, 2009

I SHALL GO MY WAY

My Boy,
On meeting you I shall go my way in peace.
True love I shall strap to my back.
For the good of man, this heart I shall share among men.

My Boy,
The power of kindness should be your tool.
Let your heart find no room for hatred.

My Boy,
Life is short.
Feed upon that which is good.
Seek and find the heart of the elders.

My Boy,
Draw from their wisdom.
God has a purpose for each one of us.
Your love, my boy, should be your light.
Let no man stop you from shining.
At this hour, the light I use to guide my hand.
Drawing from your love, the work must be done.
The lifting of the spirit I pray.

Oh! Great Sun,
As I await your face, let me pray great God for the good of man.
Help me to follow the light.
Dress me that I may lead.
True love and only true love I pray.

October 11, 2009

WHILE I LIVE

My Boy, Tristan,
While I live, something whispers within me.
Remember those eyes and take them with you.
For the good of man, crafting words I shall put this hand to use.

My Boy,
I have seen the light through the eyes of a child.

My Dear Boy,
Go forth and lead the way.
Let your love be spice to the heart.
As for me, I am full.
The working of the mind I shall direct to follow the path of love.
Sweet love, my boy, is like sweet wine to the tongue.
As I live, I shall use this tongue to taste sweet words.

My Dear Boy, Tristan,
What the world needs is love.
Nation against nation,
Man against man,
War upon war spreading its wicked face.

My Boy,
What the world needs is love.
May the power of the Most High be upon you.

My Boy,
This is the hand of a poet reaching for the hands of God.
May he take you along your journey.
Peace and love, my boy, I pray.
What the world needs is love.

October 11, 2009

131

WITH BLIND FAITH

My Boys,
I will not go without telling my story.
With blind faith,
The child from within I shall bring forth.
The sense of humanity will be my song.

My Boys,
The lust for life cannot be taken away from a living man.
With dignity I shall trod the road of destiny.
The Blessed Father gave me a song.
Such a song I shall sing to the ears of ma.
Perfect or not perfect,
My song will be my song.

Boys,
Fine-tune your ears to learn the words.
Man and his quest to please his God will embrace loneliness to
reach his goal.

My Boys,
A song of love I shall leave.
Harden not your hearts to find the will to love.

My Boys,
With humility I shall appear before your very eyes.
Oh! Take me; take me for the good of man.

October 11, 2009

GO IN PEACE

Sweet sleep, my dearly beloved.
The Father giveth and the Father taketh.
Let your work speak for you.
Heaven bound I pray.
May the angels take thee along.
Bright stars running to thee.
This is no time for tears.
A time of victory should be our cry.

My beloved, in memory of thee,
The work must be done.
The eyes of the suffering man will be taken care of.
Your work, my beloved, shall continue.
Go in peace until we meet again.

October 11, 2009

FALLEN MEN

Lady with the golden hair,
Come to me.
Come to me.
Let us go to the House of Pain.
There await the eyes of fallen men.
I shall ask of thee,
Let your beauty shine.
The mind will find a way to heal.

October 13, 2009

WHEN THE TIME IS RIGHT

My Boy,
When the time is right,
No man shall stop the meeting of the minds.
The young and old shall find a common ground.

My Boy,
I have no time to lose.

My Boy,
When the Father calls us,
The night shall turn to day.
The souls of His children shall find love.
A loving God will pilot the way.
Then and there we shall weep no more.
For the love of humanity we shall rise.
From my land to his land,
The working of the minds shall be for the good of man.
Yes, people, what a day when the two minds meet.

Father,
You have seen the desire of our hearts.
Let love be our food.
For the love of humanity,
Let me find the wisdom that this young mind may drum from I and I.

Father,
Help us to walk with thee.
The work must be done.
The eyes of the suffering man await our hands.

October 13, 2009

NO REGRETS

My Boy,
When my life ends,
There will be no regret.
When I held your hand,
I received the fire I need.
A bundle of joy coated with love,
This sets me in a new direction.

Away with hatred.
Away with earthly treasures.
The name of the game shall be true love.
Through the eyes of a child I found a new spirit.

Positive thinking shall be my cry.
In my great wealth of happiness,
The voice of a child will never leave.
A song of love I shall feed upon.
Play Grandpa. Play Grandpa.
Nice Grandpa. Nice Grandpa.
A boy using his young mind to lift the spirit of an old man.
The Good Book said a child will lead the way.

My Boy,
I shall follow your path.
May the good God lead the way.

October 13, 2009

DEEP THINKING

My Boy,
Even though you are out of sight,
My mind cannot rest.
My thoughts I shall purify for thee.
In my secret place I shall bring forth your face.
What peace I have seen.
What wind I have felt.

Power Higher Than I,
Help me to be still
Strong loves pulls me along.

My Boy,
Your face with that pleasure finds my soul that I must speak thereof.
Your name, my boy, is upon the lips of many.
I shall capture your spirit with words.

My Boy,
You came with love and you leave with love.
What could it be but the working of the Most High?
Today I will allow love to run its course.

October 13, 2009

WHY DO I WRITE?

Why do I write?
I write to taste the words from my fingers.

October 13, 2009

FORGIVENESS

My Boys,
If you cannot forgive,
You will not find time to rest.
The heart will be a burden to carry.

October 13, 2009

WHY DO I SING?

Who do I sing?
I sing because it brings peace to the soul.
A happy heart will attract the eyes of others.
Man and his troubled mind await healing.
A sweet tune excites the heart.
A heart that beats with love will be a blessing to others.

October 13, 2009

TRUE AFFECTION

My Dear,
I shall learn to love thee.
True affection will come to thee.
A loving heart will beat for thee.
Let no false lips jump for thee.
What is yours is yours.
Well, then,
Let the river run its course.
If thirst should find thee,
Go and fill thyself.

October 14, 2009

LET US GO IN PEACE

Awake, my spirit.
Awake, my spirit.
The eyes of the boy await thee.

Father,
You have seen the journey take me along.
How long shall I weep for the meeting of the minds?

My Friends,
Grandstanding I do not need.
Face to face I shall stand.
True love, my friends, I pray.
Blood to blood will be our cry.
Let our eyes be fixed.

Great God,
You have seen the desire of our hearts.
For the good of man,
Lift up our spirits.
Let us walk hand in hand.

My Boy,
What is to be must be.
The power of payers will move all obstacles.
You came to this land for a purpose.
Blessed are the peacemakers.
The Good Book said a child will lead the way.

My Boy,
Rise up and do your Father's work.
The work must be done.
Let us go in peace.

October 14, 2009

THE RISE AND FALL OF MAN

You might not need me,
But you never can tell.
Well, then, boast not of your standing.
I have seen the rise and fall of man.
Today when I look at man who fell from grace,
All I can see is madness.

My Friends,
Be humble along your journey.
Heap no shame upon others.
Remember the rise and fall of man.
Here today, and tomorrow nowhere to be found.

October 14, 2009

139

BOYS, BEAR WITH ME

My Boys,
Bear with me.
I have to share the love.
I cannot lean on one then lean away from the other.
You are both precious to me.

Blessed Father,
You have seen these two boys.
They are my blood.
How could I not love them?
You both allowed me to focus the mind.

My Boys,
Sweet words I pray to find.

My Boys,
If suffering will allow me to live a good life,
The torch I beg you both to carry along.
Good deeds, my boys, I pray.
This is the voice of an old man reaching for the ears of two boys.

My Boys,
If I did not find that love,
Why would I need this hand?

Boys,
I am the captain of my journey.
I shall ride on the back of dignity.

October 14, 2009

BOYS, GO INTO THE WORLD

My Boys,
I know that I am going in the right direction.
Not many men will leave their hands.
As for me,
Here are my hands.
It's an honor to present the workhorse.
For the good of man,
I have done my best.
The rest time will tell.
May history be kind to them.

My Boys,
Let us unite our hearts for the good of man.
I need your young minds to work upon that which is good.

My Boys,
The world needs some good hands.

My Boys,
Even though this world is full of unfulfilled people,
Find the courage to take the words to them.

Boys,
Fix your minds upon the true God.
Then go into the world and do His work.

October 14, 2009

LIKE DUST

When I look at the weakness of man,
I pity the boastful tongue.
Man is like dust awaiting the winds.
Here today and nowhere to be found tomorrow.

October 15, 2009

COMMUNICATION

My Boys,
I shall allow truth to bring forth a form of communication,
One that I shall direct on behalf of true love.
Love is that great inner feeling that feeds the heart,
A bundle of peace that lifts the spirit.
If you feed a child upon that which is good,
Such a child will produce that which is good.

My Boys,
I shall reach out for your young minds.
What the world needs is love.
Nation against nation.
Man against man.

My God,
When will it end?
When will man find the will to love?

Father,
In your name I present these two boys.
True love and only true love I pray.

Holy Father,
Lay your hands upon these two boys.
The soul of humanity awaits them.
Peace and love I pray.

October 15, 2009

WHEN WILL IT END?

My Boy,
In my study your picture generates peace.
A poet finding peace, his mind will be clear,
His thoughts sweet and clean.
Today I humbly ask the Blessed Father to guide my hands.

My Boy,
Without Him I am nothing.
For the love of humanity,
I will not give sleep to my eyes.

My Boy,
I am a workhorse for the good of man.

Father,
In this time of great need,
The plight of man is upon the land.
A nation so mighty in battle,
Yet its people beg for mercy.
The suffering man cannot find a place to rest.

My God, My God,
When will it end?
The rich getting richer and the poor getting poorer.

My God,
When will it end?

October 16, 2009

TENDER VOICE

My Boy,
Your tender voice finds the rhythm of this heart.
Oh, come to me!
Come, my boy, let me find your eyes.
May the good Lord bless you.

My Boy,
You are on a mission of peace.
Let the love from thee be a comfort to others.

My Boy,
In the sight of God,
Bring out the beauty from within.
Let those with eyes see that you are from a living God.
Let there be no limit to your true love.
Stay in a charming state that you may win the hearts of others.

My Boy,
Along life's journey,
Focus on discipline.
Let your feet find dignity.
When this is done,
I shall not be troubled.

October 16, 2009

GREAT SUFFERINGS

Holy Father,
I stand before thee as the sun rises.
Eastbound I look on.
For the good of man, I beg of thee.
Let me find words that will cool the heart.
In this time of great sufferings,
The weeping of a nation is on the move.
Peace and prosperity are nowhere in sight.
The suffering of a people drove some to madness.

Father,
Are they not your children?
Your mercy I pray.

Father,
Let men find the will to live again.
Deep courage and faith I beg of thee.
Where are the Good Shepherds?

Power Higher Than I,
Let the people rejoice again.
Show unto us they mercy.

October 16, 2009

THE POWER OF WORDS

My Boy,
At this hour I feel the power of words feeding upon my soul.

Blessed Father,
Help me to be calm.
Help this hand to work for thee.
Now that my mind is fresh,

Father,
Hear my cry.
For the good of man let me find sweet words.
I have seen men not knowing who they are.
The working of the mind is beyond my control.

Blessed Father,
Comforting words would be a blessing to the soul.

My Boy,
Come with your young hands that we may do the Father's work.
Use your sweet voice to charm the hearts.
Sweet music, my boy, is like food to the soul.
Sing, my boy, that I may sing along.
Oh! Wondering eyes, fret not thyself.
Seek and find the hands of the Good Shepherds.
Step from the dark into the light.

My Boy,
When my hands no longer work.
Let your voice be heard.
Go to the heart of the suffering man.

My Boy,
Today I come in peace.
May true love be upon you.

October 16, 2009

IN GOD'S NAME

In God's name he is one of God's children.
Why is he not fee to walk upon God's lane?
Who are you to own this land?
This land is your receiver.
Do not be a fool and lose your cool.
We are all God's children.
Who are you to poke fun at His creation?

October 16, 2009

YOUR CHILDREN

Awake, my spirit!
The words to live by are upon me.
In this time of great suffering,
Comforting words are worth fine gold.
Man in his quest to live,
Will feed upon the words.

Great God,
Let honor return to thee.
Man in his plight of great pain has no choice.
His pride is of no use.
In shame he will find his knees.
Then pour out his heart seeking forgiveness.

Father,
Have mercy upon your children.

October 16, 2009

AT THE MOUNTAIN

My Boy,
At this hour I am with the mountain a wiser man.
Clear as crystal, the heavens in its glory.
Fading stars returning to their rightful place.
The moon, even though half-full, fading away.
The sun, my boy, is not yet upon me.

My Boy,
The pleasure ahead I shall await to warm my spirit.
I came to the mountain with an open mind, not knowing that
man would present himself.
What peace have I encountered?
At left, a fallen man searched the garbage for what is left.
Man in a state of hunger pulls the hardest of heart.
What pity finds my breast?
A beautiful morning ruined by human suffering.

My Boy,
I could not control mine eyes not to look.
The fall of man lines the heart with sadness.

My Boy,
The hardness of the heart could not find room.

My Boy,
I do not know what came over me.

October 17, 2009

148

DO SOMETHING

My Boys,
At this break of dawn I rise.
Let me find my knees.

Great God,
Let me be thankful to see another day.
For the good of man, may my years be a blessing.

My Boys,
I shall seek thy young hearts.
For the good of man, I beg you both to lend a helping hand.

Boys,
Do not be proud.
Remember we are all God's children.
Forget not the common man.

Boys,
From my youth I have dedicated my years towards service.
Much is expected of you both.

Boys,
Find the will to do good.
Harden not your hearts against the suffering man.

Boys,
As I await the sun, so shall I await your hands.

Blessed Father,
You have seen that I have gone to my soul.
The burden of man rests upon me.
I shall go to the mountain to seek knowledge and wisdom.
Let nature in its glory be my guide.

October 17, 2009

MY BOY, BE GRATEFUL

My Boy,
Be grateful to the elder for his wit to inspire.
A Godly man will reach for his God,
Knowing that through him all things are possible.
Wisdom, my boy, does not come overnight.
The dedication of ones heart will lead him to the House of Wisdom.

My Boy,
Humility is the key to success.
The blessed Father knows his servant.

My Boy,
You have a mind of your own.
Find the ears of the elder and learn his craft.
It is better to be late than stay idle.

October 17, 2009

INDULGENCE

My Boy,
I beg for your indulgence.
Come to these old hands.
How long, how long have I awaited thee?
Let me pull out the gift of love.
Your eyes, my boy, I shall bless with mine.
Are you not my blood?
Well, then, who are those hands?
No amount of hands shall stop the meeting of the minds.

My Boy,
Let true love put their eyes to shame.
Come, my boy, sing with me.
Play Grandpa, play Grandpa.
Nice Grandpa, nice Grandpa.
The capturing of the spirits are in the making.

My Boy,
When the Divine One lays his hands,
Who is man to stand in the way?
Let us line our path with true love.
Allow the eyes to make a note of our journey.

My Boy,
By all means, let our light shine.
Let our minds enroll them.

October 17, 2009

TODAY

Blessed Father,
Here I am.
I cannot wait to find the hands of these two boys.
Oh! Journey, when shall I begin?
Alone I ponder my path.
How my soul longs for their eyes.
Today I cannot rest.
The hands of time I follow.
Sweet words I shall mix for their taste.

Boys,
Whatever you do,
Remember my hands will be yours.
Today the gladness of my heart finds the back of the winds.
Awake my spirit.
The eyes of the boys await I and I.

Great Father,
Clearance I pray.
No journey, no distance shall entrap my spirit.
My mind is bent on fixing mine eyes.

Holy Father,
Today I feel the urge to go forth.
Spur me that I may gallop with love sealed to my heart,
A heart that I will share among my boys.

Father,
Today, today, I call upon thee.
Hear my cry for victory.
The testing of faith I shall ensure.

October 17, 2009

LET US REJOICE

My Boy,
Let us rejoice together.
Let us give praises to the Most High.
Oh, what a beautiful morning!
Let us bind our love.
Before sunrise I have to go.

My Boy,
I came in peace,
And I found love.
Who could it be but the Holy Father?
Even though you are young at heart,
You have a mind of your own.

Blessed Father,
You have seen the meeting of the minds.
Let us follow the right path.

My Boy,
From our happiness,
Let us work for the good of man.

October 17, 2009

WHY MUST I RUN?

My Dear,
Why must I run after thee?
When I have extended my hands,
Have you not eyes to see?
Pulling tears are too much for the eyes.
Come, let us find a common ground.
For the good of man,
Your hands would be a blessing.
All night long sleep would not come,
Yet the work must go on.

October 17, 2009

IN SILENCE

My Boy,
If you find the gift of love.
Go and share it among your people.

My Boy,
What the world needs is love.
Have great courage for the suffering man.
I have seen man eating dirt while other turn their heads.

My Boy,
Be kind to the fallen man.

My Boy,
Respect the value of time.
Remember time awaits no man.
Let the gladness of your heart lift your spirit.

My Boy,
One needs a strong spirit to fight in justice.
You are a product of this land.
No one can take you away.
Well, then, stand up and let your voice be heard.

As for me,
I need not boast of my stand.
I asked the great God for his blessing,
Seeking his ears that I may do greater things.
What I do today,
May others find some comfort.

My Boy,
I am too far gone now.
The light I shall leave for you to carry.
In silence let me pray.

October 18, 2009

LET US RISE UP

Come to me, my boy.
Come to your blood.
Do not be afraid of these hands.
I have washed them for thee.
These are the hands I lifted up to the Most High.

My Boy,
A higher power is at work.
Our eyes were meant to find our souls.

My Boy,
The peace of God is upon us.
From this day I shall write for thee.

Blessed Father,
Help me to find words to capture his spirit.
A smiling face beaming with pure love I shall recreate.
Oh, wondering eyes, he is mine!
Come sing with us and give thanks for the meeting of the minds.

My Boy,
You and I shall find the will to serve.
For the good of man,
Let us rise up,
Then find the courage to do our Father's work.

October 18, 2009

TIME WILL TELL / TRISTAN / TANNER

My Boys,
As the sun rises,
I shall allow my thoughts to ride on the back of the wind.

Blessed Father,
Teach me the heart of communication.
These two young minds I shall work with.

Boys,
For the love of humanity,
I pray that you may find the will to serve.
A loving heart will bring success.
Well, then, allow me to speak to you both.

My Boys,
As the sun serves its purpose to this world,
Let your lives and let your lights shine.
Seek and find the path of the Good Shepherds.
I shall teach love for all mankind.
If you teach a child to feed upon that which is good,
One prays that such a child will produce that which is good.

My Boys,
Today I look beyond the sun.
Your names I take along.
The hands of God I beg for his mercy.
Long life, my boys, I pray.
For the good of man,
I pray for your young minds.

Boys,
Now that I have exposed my emotions,
Let me go on my journey.

My Boys,
If I teach you well,
Time will tell my dreams.

October 18, 2009

THE HEART OF A CHILD

My Boy,
Stay with me.
Let me clean my hands.
I shall focus on God's words.
"A child shall lead the way."

My Boy,
You have cleared a path for me.
With your face in my memory,
I shall run with the words.
Oh! Men of great suffering,
Come and feed upon the food.
Come, my people, if you are in need.

Blessed Father,
For those in need,
Take charge of their weary hearts.

Father,
Unto thee I present my findings.
Let me find thy ears.
Let man find the will to love again.
Fatten their hears that they may praise thee again.

Oh! Loving God,
Remember your children.

October 18, 2009

x

IN MY SECRET PLACE

My Boy,
Alone in my secret place,
My mind is set on thee,
Your picture on the wall finding my soul.
I shall go within my soul for thee.

Let me pray.
Blessed Father, you have seen the desire of this heart.
The eyes of this boy will never leave.
Holy Father, bless his years.
May he rise up to give of himself.
Lord, help me to shape his young mind,
To feed upon that which is good.
Blessed Father, I am willing to become an active teacher in his life.
I have seen the love in this boy,
A boy filled with life,
A caring boy that is willing to share his love.
Not in my many years have I seen such a child.
Father, you must have touched him,
A boy that is willing to sing to the weary souls.
May he strive with such courage for the good of man.
Blessed Father, help this boy to walk with the light.
Along his journey, may the gladness of his heart bring joy to others.
How could I not find time to pray for this boy?

My Boy,
I have seen myself in you.
I have seen your tender hands.
From my secret place I now call upon a Higher Power.
Power Higher than I,
May this boy trod upon a clear path.
True love, my boy, I pray.

October 19, 2009

NAMES OF THE DEAD

My Friends,
I am among the names of the dead.
To the East I pray.
Dripping tears I shall leave to mark my spot.
Wandering feet pulling the eyes.
The hands of evil let loose upon the land.

Great God,
You have seen the work of evil men,
Men turning themselves into a pillow of fire,
Leaving names upon names at the rock.
In memory of the dead,
The living came to mourn.
What sorrows have I seen?

My God,
I come to thee this morning.
May these names be in your book.
Down on my knees I pray for peace.
Soften the hearts of the living that peace may be upon their hearts.
Today I pray.
Let us find the will to love again.
May these lost souls find favor with thee.

October 23, 2009

THE BATTLE PLAN

My Boy,
You have shaped my thoughts.
Now I am on a new course.

My Boy,
A child shall lead the way.
Through your love, the sign of peace is at hand.
From your hand to my hand,
The lifting of hands praising the true God.
Your name is upon their lips.

My Boy,
Use your young mind to do your father's work.
You are on a mission of peace.
No one can stop you now.
The sweetness of your voice has captured the hearts of many.

My Boy,
I thank you for your goodness.
Yes, my boy, I shall pray for your courage.
My years I shall dedicate towards your growth.

My Boy,
With full eyes you allow me to see the light.
I shall not allow these fingers to rest.
The world shall see your good work.

October 23, 2009

MY FRIENDS

My Friends,
In this time of great sorrow,
I shall be your cane.
Lean on me that I may take you along.

My Friends,
Your pain shall be my pain.
What are friends for?
A true friend will not turn his back.
If there is fire,
He will seek water.
In the name of friendship,
One should be true to his calling.

October 23, 2009

IF YOU SHOULD LEAVE

My Dear,
If you should break my heart,
I shall ask of thee not in public.
Let the good times outlast the bad times.
If you should leave,
Let the dark cover your face.
Spare me the excitement of the heart.

October 23, 2009

I CAME TO YOU

I cam to you not knowing who you are.
Let peace be upon us.
Let the gladness of my heart find favor with you.
Your pain shall be my pain.
Your tears shall be mine.
Here are my hands.
Come walk with me.
Let me be your cane.
Do not be afraid.
Everything will be alright.
Power higher than I,
Today I call upon thee.
Let your hands be upon us.

October 24, 2009

THE VOICE OF AN ANGEL

My Dear,
What sweetness finds this heart.
Oh! Wind be kind to me.
Be still and allow my ears its rhythm.
The voice of an angel must be passing by.

October 24, 2009

COME TO THESE HANDS

Come, my boy, come to these old hands.
Do not be afraid; they are yours.
I will not allow strange hands the pleasure.
I will teach you about life.
I have seen a lot in my years.
Your eyes should feed upon that which is good.
A clean heart will create wonders.
My boy, I will assure you of these hands.
Give unto me the rhythm I need.

October 24, 2009

WHAT LIPS

My Dear,
What lips have I seen?
The sweet voice to me is like music to the ears.
Move them that I may sing along.

October 24, 2009

TEACH US THY WAYS

My Boy,
Your love lifted me up.
I am now a new man.
I shall go my way with a happy spirit.
For the love of humanity I shall use this burning love
to charm the hearts.

My Boy,
You came at a time when men were losing the will to live.
A nation under great strain.
Wars upon wars.
Mothers who were once proud,
Now beaten down with great sorrows.
The names of the dead pulling tears from the hardest hearts.

My Boy,
What the world needs is love.

My God,
Let us as a people find the will to love again.
I have seen love jumping all over this boy.
How could I not return his love?

Blessed Father, help me to share the love.
Let me find words to dress with love.
What the world needs is love.

Blessed Father, you are the father of true love.
Teach us thy ways.

October 24, 2009

164

I SHALL FIND TIME

My Boy,
Now I am alone.
I shall find time to serve thee.
Your picture I shall look at.
From memory I shall speak about our eyes.
Eyes to eyes we stand.
The old and young minds allow our spirits to be at peace.

My Boy,
Let us work for the good of man.
If I feed your young mind upon that which is good,
I pray that you will go and do your Father's work.

October 24, 2009

A HUMBLE MAN

Blessed Father,
Today I come to thee a humble man.
As I await the face of the sun,
The face of my boy I shall await.

Father,
Let no journey, no distance dampen my spirit.
In your name I lifted up his young mind.
For the good of man let us unite to do your work.
I have seen the eyes of suffering men longing for some good hands.

Father,
Today I went deep within.
Your hands I prayed to find.
The burden of man caught mine eyes.

Father,
Let me find the will to serve.
Let me find the wisdom to teach this boy.
I have seen the love in his eyes.
Let him follow the path of the Good Shepherds.
Let his young mind produce that which is good.

Father,
From my secret place I present my case.
Let me go in peace.

October 24, 2009

PRAISES

My Boy,
It is my desire to give praises.
I believe a man should give thanks for his years.
A man should live a life that pleases his God.
A man should live a life that others may follow.
A man should be his brother's keeper.
A man in his quest for life should live and let others live.
A man should allow good deeds to be his trademark.
A man only lives once.
History should be able to find his name.
A man and his moral principles should be a lesson that others
may learn.
As for me, let me be thankful for lending a hand.
The eyes of the suffering man I could not escape.

My God,
I have done my best.
The working of the mind I shall use for the good of man.

October 24, 2009

GAIN YOUR WINGS

My Boy,
Forgive me of my hands.
The working of the mind took a hold of them.

My Boy,
I cannot take my music with me.
Well, then, I shall fine-tune it for thee.
Use your young ears to be attentive.
The voice of an old man cries out to thee.
The suffering man rests upon this heart.

My Boy,
I shall weep no more.
I have done my best.
I and I cannot carry the weight.

My Boy,
If I teach you well,
Use your youthfulness to fight for a just cause.
Set your eyes upon the prize.
Then lean forward to gain your wings.

October 25, 2009

WHERE ARE YOU?

If I should cry,
I would cry for my Mother.
Oh! Mother, Mother, where are you?
If I should sing,
I would sing for my Mother.
Mother, where are you?
Dreams upon dreams you came.
My nights are yours.
I shall not be afraid.
Your tender hands will never leave.

October 25, 2009

VANITY

My Boy,
I shall not lead my soul to vanity.
I am worthy of better things.
I shall not trade my soul for fine gold.
Well, then, the burden of man I shall lend a hand.
A loving heart I pray to keep.

My Boy,
Great faith I shall allow roots.

October 25, 2009

YOU ARE MY EYES

My Love,
Come to me.
Come let us reason.
Allow me to speak.
You are my eyes and ears.
Without you I cannot see clearly.

Well, then, I shall cry to thee.
Hear are my hands.
Take what is yours.
For the love of humanity, let's pledge our years.

My Love,
Work with me.
The work must be done.
Let us rise up for the good of man.

October 25, 2009

COMPASSION

Finding compassion towards others,
One needs to bear that pity with a loving heart.
A person in need should not escape your eyes.
A good man will allow his spirit the gift of love.
Within his heart a good deed will be his cry.
Great hope will feed his thoughts.
Finding compassion one needs to tap the soul.
The goodness of his heart will be his tools for the job.
My brothers and sister,
Let us find the will to be kind.

October 28, 2009

WHERE ARE THE HUMAN EYES?

Where are all the human eyes?
Father, I come before your very eyes.
For the good of man, let me rise to find the suffering eyes.
Father, their tears I cannot hold.
The head of man is not what it used to be.

Father, a bold spirit I beg of thee.
Let me not harden this heart.
Let me find the desire to do your work.
The weeping of man is too much for the soul.
From my secret place I call to thee.
Let me find the will to serve.
Today I present this heart.
Lead me on the journey.
The eyes of a fallen man dreaming on.
Awake, my spirit.
Awake, my spirit.
Let us go to the heart of the fallen man.

October 28, 2009

MY BROTHERS AND SISTERS

My Brothers and Sisters,
When you look at man in a state of suffering,
The calling of the heart cannot be left unfulfilled.
Man in a state of weakness should not escape the eyes.
Remember the strong should help the weak,
That the weak may become strong.

My Brothers and Sisters,
Stand up and do that which is good.

October 29, 2009

THY LIPS

My Dear,
Thy lips are like honey.
What sweetness have I sipped from?
Now let me be calm.
Let me allow the gladness of this heart to beat for thee.

My Friends,
Come rejoice with me.
Today I stand to face the music.
What is mine is mine.
The Lord giveth and the Lord taketh.

October 29, 2009

FROM MY WEARY EYES

From my weary eyes the hands of evil made my heart as hard as a rock.
I watched the once happy man lifting his first to God.
The smell of death was upon the land.
My God, let me hide mine eyes from this madness.
No voice could lift my spirit.
When will this madness cease?
Dear Lord, forget us not.

October 30, 2009

SLEEP NOT

Love, sleep not until death finds its course.
Let your eyes await mine.

October 30, 2009

I AM NOT THE SAME

My Boy,
Since I met you,
I am not the same.
My mind cannot rest.
Love and peace took a hold of me.
The lessons I learned,
I shall use for the good of man.
A little love will serve as a boost to the soul.
Man in a state of misery will be thankful to find a loving hand.
Through the eyes of a child,
The message of love finds a receiving heart.

October 30, 2009

LAUGHTER

I love to hear your laughter.
What sweetness finds the ears.
A happy soul in full blast.
Day by day the ears await their laughter.
My friends, laughter is a good thing go shape the face.

October 30, 2009

OUR SWEETNESS

My Dear,
Our sweetness shall not go to waste.
Let our seeds be prepared to rise up.

October 30, 2009

PEACE AND LOVE

My Boys, to find peace there must be love.

If love cannot find a seat at the table,
My Boys, peace will not be seen.

October 30, 2009

THE WORK OF THE HANDS

Come, My Friends,
Let us put our hands together.
For the good of man, let us unit to fight for a just cause.
The suffering of man needs a cheerful giver.

My Friends,
Harden not your hearts.
Today for me, tomorrow for you.
Let the goodness of your heart lift the spirit of the suffering man.
Today I come to you with a broken heart.
Mine eyes have seen enough.
When will it end?
When will the suffering man find the joy to love again?
When will his eyes be right?

My Friends,
Allow compassion to fail not.

My Friends,
How can we not grieve for the suffering man?
Mine eyes affected my heart.

Blessed Father,
Bless the work of these hands.

October 30, 2009

THE SEEDS OF VIOLENCE

My boys, I will not allow you to grow the seeds of violence.
I shall take it upon myself to teach the heart of true love.
My boys, you both are a part of me.
True peace I shall preach.
My boys, promise me now that Grandpa will be proud.
My boys, what this world needs is compassion.
We are all God's children.

Boys, feed upon love that you may share with others.
I have seen the hands of hatred.
Man finding hatred that madness took a hold of him.
My boys, use your minds for the good of man.
My boys, a loving heart can create wonders.
Let the spirits of the ancestors find thee.
As for me, I shall shape my hands for you both.

Boys, allow me to reason with the child from within.
A mother's love will never leave.
For the love of humanity, boys, feed upon the teaching of your parents.
The only weapon you shall carry is love.
True love, my boys, will break the heart of a violent man.
My boys, be willing to open your hearts to the suffering man.
Cover not your eyes to escape reality.
Remember we are all God's children.
Love and only love shall be my cry.

November 1, 2009

THE JOY OF LIVING

My Boys,
The joy of living is to find the deepest love.
Then allow it to pull you along your journey.
A loving heart will find its beat.
Sail on, my dear boys.
Keep the fire burning.
A cold heart will not find its flame.

November 2, 2009

DAY BY DAY

Day by day I rise to face the task ahead.
If not dead, life goes on.
The rise and fall will never end.
Life along its journey, no one knows its end.
A man should chart his course.
A man should give allowance to the winds.
My friends, sometimes strong winds take you off course.
Find the courage to press on.
A great achiever will dedicate his time to climb that mountain.
A man in his quest to leave this world a better place will allow
good reason to dictate his path.
If a man does not have a dream, what stream will he find?
Clear waters, my friends, are a beauty to the eyes.
Its mighty flow will stimulate the mind.
A man who reasons in peace will find love.
My friends, pity me not.
I shall follow my calling.
Great dreams are yet to be told.
Yes, my friends, let history speak thereof.

November 2, 2009

INSTRUCTIONS

My Boy,
What struck me was that look upon your face,
A face that would calm the heart of a dying man.
As for me, I have found a new spirit to live.
I shall set the record straight.
I will not go down before I leave my hands for you.

My Boy,
It is hard for me not to frame my thoughts.
The common man will need your hands.
Go to school, my boy.
At the seat of higher learning feed upon knowledge that wisdom
may be your tool.
For the good of man, cut loose the forces of race.
Remember, my boy, we are all God's children.
Waste not your youth.
Find the will to serve.
Good deeds, my boy, will be a blessing.

I shall leave you now.
Go and do your Father's work.
Remember the work must be done.

November 2, 2009

TANNER

My Dear Boy Tanner,
Early to rise to await the face of the sun.
Let me pray.
Holy Father, here I am.
My thoughts are upon this boy.
Let me live that our eyes may greet each other.

My dear boy, from the mother's breast fatten your little heart.
What is to be will be.
The Father of all fathers will lead the way.
How I long to greet thee.
Awake, my spirit.
Awake, my spirit.
The eyes of the boy I shall await.

Oh! Great sun, your face I have seen.
Father, let me find the courage to look beyond the sun.
Oh! Great Master of the Universe,
At this hour I call upon thee.
Let me find the face of this boy.
Let my love foster our friendship.
He is my blood.
How could I not love him?

Father, today I look to the East.
The face of the sun I have seen clearly.
The face of this boy I shall await.
Spirit of mine be still.
Let me expose my emotions.

November 3, 2009

ALL IS WELL WITH ME

My Boys,
This is the dead of night.
Sweet sleep will not come.
Let me set my thoughts upon the words.

My Boys,
All is well with me.
I shall make use of the time I am awake.

Boys,
All by myself the working of the mind I shall put to use.
The roads leading to your hearts I shall commit to memory.
Oh! Happy soul, let me plant my seeds.
Under this full moon I shall wish upon the stars.

The Blessed Father is in my head.
Father, let the stillness of the night help me find moments
of real blessing.
The sweetness of life I shall take to the heart of these two boys.
Let us unit in love.

Blessed Father,
Quicken me to find their eyes.
Now that I have lifted my heart to thee,
Bless these hands that I may carry the words.
If I cannot learn from the stillness of the night,
May sleep take a hold of these eyes.

My Boys,
I find true joy writing for the both of us.
May the power of love lift me from the dark to see the light.

My Boys,
From my secret place I shall allow peace and love to shut mine eyes.

November 4, 2009

HUMAN MISERY

Oh! Lamb of God,
Take my weary soul to the rock that is higher than I.
Human misery lets me feel like an empty man.
I shall gaze upon the sun,
Then put my thoughts in order.
I shall call upon a Higher Power to lead me along.
Beyond my wildest dreams,
The burden of man took a hold of me.

November 4, 2009

MY BOYS, I SHALL SPEAK

My Boys,
I shall speak from this heart from my secret place,
One stray cat looks upon me.
Its eyes and mine cannot be moved.
Even though wild in nature,
She took time out to fend for herself.
How could I not break bread with her?
Each day I look forward to seeing her.

My Boys,
What friendship I have seen.

My Boys,
Find the will to love.
Do good and good will follow you.
For the love of humanity,
Let the spirits of your ancestors be proud.
As for me, please hear my cry.
Find the light and allow your hearts to walk with the light.

My Boys,
I shall find my knees for the both of you.
As I follow the hands of time,
I shall frame my thought for your young hearts.
The cat and I bid farewell.

My Boys,
If I teach you well,
Time will tell of my hands.

November 5, 2009

AT THE BREAK OF DAWN

My Boy,
What a happy day.
At the break of dawn,
The meeting of the minds was in full view.
Man and boy touched the heart of the Good Shepherds.
Oh! What a happy day.
The angels must be singing.

My Boy,
Who could it be but the working of the blessed Father?
Tim, my boy, is the master of everything.

Holy Father,
This morning I am before you a humble man.
You have seen the desire of this heart.
Love and only true love I bring.
Can a man run from his blood?
No valley, no mountain will contain his spirit.

Blessed Father,
When you hands are at work,
The work must be done.
Oh! Great sun from your light,
Man and boy shall trod upon a clear path.

My Lord,
On this great day,
I beg of thee,
Seal our love that we may walk with thee.
Let me find the wisdom that I may teach this boy.

My Boy,
No tears shall find us.
Let us be thankful for this day.

November 5, 2009

MY PRIDE AND DREAMS

My Boys,
My pride and dreams I shall leave in words.
The purity of the soul I shall not dilute.
Even though my fingers are laden with pain,
I will not leave my love alone.
An honest mind I shall put on display.
In silence I shall find my knees.

True God, in your name I come.
Let the working of this mind produce that which is good.
On the subject of love,
Let me find the ways to teach these boys.
In my old glory, Father, let me pray.

Love I cannot leave alone.
Man to man is unjust.
The hands of hatred are upon the land.
Peace and love should be upon the lips of man.
If you feed a child upon that which is good,
Such a child will produce that which is good.

My Boys,
In the name of peace and love,
It's me, not your father,
Not your mother,
Not your brother.
It's me, your Grandpa.
Let the working of this old mind be for the good of man.

November 6, 2009

OUT OF MYSELF – TRISTAN

My Boy,
At this moment in time,
I shall get out of myself.

My Boy,
Until my journey is done,
The working of the mind I shall share with you.

My Boy,
I shall allow the memory of your voice to sing in my head.
Let it mock this heart with true love while I fill myself with great joy.
For the good of man I shall allow the freedom of love to guide my path.
Take my hands and let us walk with the light.
Stay with me and let us reason.
If I am unkind to thee,
Forget this hand of mine.

My Boy,
When I am gone,
Take this hand to the heart of the children.
Forget not my dreams for the good of man.
Let my spirit find thee.

My Boy,
You will be my eyes and ears.
Remember where my heart lives.
Remember what I stood for.

My Boy,
Remember that on this day I came out of my soul to reason with you.
Peace and love I bring to thee.

November 7, 2009

LEAVE NOT MY HANDS UNTOUCHED

My Boys,
If I should go in a hurry,
Leave not my hands untouched.
Day by day I took time out to prepare them.
The shaping of words took a toll upon them.
Sleeping fingers I have to awake.
Running thoughts I have to redirect.
Focus, my boys, I put into practice.
The work must be done.
How could I allow my years to go to waste?
What comfort would I leave for your young hearts?
Well, then, my boys,
Let me do what I love to do.
May the words I find dance upon your tongues.

My Boys,
Roll them for the good of man.
Take them to the heart of the suffering man.
If one soul finds peace,
The working of my hands would be a blessing.
On this day I could not control my raw emotions.
The words came with fire.

My Boys,
Look for the light.
Let your hearts follow the light.

November 7, 2009

THE HUMAN SOUL

My Boy,
When I look at the human soul,
What pity I bear.
Man in his quest for fine gold forgets that the earth awaits his remains.
How long, my Lord, shall the hands of evil spread?
Where have the good men gone?
By love they shall return.
If I may, from my secret place,
Let me speak my mind before it's too late.
Great faith I shall feed upon.
The soul of humanity I pray.

My Brothers and Sisters,
In the name of humanity let peace and love find its course.
Oh, wind! The birds came along with sweet songs.
May the heart of man find its rhythm.

My Brothers and Sisters,
Forgive me of my hands.
The burden of man rests upon them.

November 7, 2009

HOW PROUD I AM

My Boy,
The message I am hearing from you is one of true love.
Who am I not to follow your wish?

My Boy,
You have found the will to love.
Who am I not to spread the joy?
The gladness of this heart I shall take to the eyes of man.

Blessed Father,
You have seen this boy find the will to lead.
Walk with him that he may do the work.
In the name of true love,
The work must be done.
The voice of a child cried out for peace.
When I consider how my days are spent,
With all my heart, I am thankful for this boy.
In silence from my secret place I feel the spirit of good leading the way.

My Boy,
If you please,
Here are my hands.
Let us walk the streets of love.
How proud I am.

November 7, 2009

GRANT UNTO US

Grandson,
I cannot tell why you cry for me.
I work this mind to read your young mind.
It must be something good.
Keep on doing what you're doing, my boy.
The working of the Lord will clear the path.

All is well with me.
Your love will never leave.
Day by day you find maturity.
I shall await your young eyes.
The meeting of the minds will focus on good old times.
Then and there we shall play again.
Your sweet voice will find this heart again.
Singing, "Play, Grandpa. Play, Grandpa."
"Nice Grandpa. Nice Grandpa."

Oh! Blessed Father, you have seen the desire of our hearts.
Grant unto us the food we need.

November 8, 2009

IN THE NAME OF PEACE

In the name of peace I call upon all men of conscience.
Let us find the will to give the peace sign.
Peace, my brother.
Peace, my sister.
Today in good faith, one love.
My people, in the name of peace, stand up.
Let your fingers do the work.
Peace, my brother.
Peace, my sister.

November 8, 2009

I LOVE THEE

My Boy,
I love thee with a love of Grandpa's love,
A love that feeds my heart with joy.
Now I shall take time out to mediate upon thee.
Such journey, my boy, I only had fond memories.
I could not love thee without honor.
How sweet it feels to remember thy face.
I have been greeted with an innocent love,
A love made in heaven.
How could I not give praises to the Blessed Father?

My Boy,
It is well with me.
What human gift have I received?

My Boy,
On the Lord's Day,
I shall find words to honor thee.
Holy Father, in your name I present the face of this boy.
Bless him that he may be a poster child for love.
Let the light from his eyes find the weary hearts.

November 9, 2009

A PEACEFUL HEART

My Boy,
From my bed I shall write for thee.
A peaceful heart I shall take to thee.
Alone I am at my best.
My thoughts are sweet to me.
Sweet music blended with love pulling my ears.
When I remember your young voice,
My spirit is on alert.
My mind is working out the words I need.
A song of love rests upon me.

Great Master of the Universe,
I look to find running stars.
I shall wish upon their tails.
A song of love composed in Heaven,
I will take to the ears of man.
A boy with his sweet voice will sing along.

Angel of Mercy,
Here I am.
Let the meditation of my heart feed upon the words I need.
A song of love I pray to find.

November 9, 2009

THE MOUNTAIN

My Boy,
I shall leave this troubled place and go to the mountain.
There I shall find peace.
I shall look at nature in its glory.
The sun I shall await.
Singing birds I shall view from a distance.
I shall unwind my dreams.

My Boy,
In the presence of dancing trees,
I shall use this mind for the good of man.
In peace I shall work my thoughts to find comforting words.
What this world needs is love.
Oh! Mountain, here are the eyes that find thee.
I am who I am,
The hands of a poet reaching for the heavens.

November 9, 2009

SPEAK AND I SHALL LISTEN

My Boy,
My ears are at your service.
Speak and I shall listen with keen ears.
Share your thoughts with this old man.

My Boy,
I have lived a long life.
I have seen many things.
Life and its journey are not a bed of roses.
Sometimes up, sometimes down.
The good and the bad will always cross paths.

My Boy,
One needs a cool head.
Strong faith, my boy, is a must.
A clean heart, my boy, will allow you to feed upon that which is good.
Train your young mind to follow the path of the Good Shepherds.
Stay away from hatred.
A heavy heart is not good for the soul.
Feed upon the words that you may walk with God.
Do not be afraid to seek knowledge.
Respect your elders and draw from their wisdom.
As for me,
The knowledge I gained, I shall share with you.

My Boy,
Live and let others live.
Share the goodness of your heart with others.
Good deeds, my boy, are like spice to the soul.

My Boy,
By the mountain where I sat,
I allowed this heart to be in tune with nature.

November 9, 2009

LET US BE READY

Come, my boy, let us find time to reason.
For the love of humanity, let us be humanlike.
Let us seek and find the path of the Good Shepherds.

My boy, good deeds shall be our burden.
Let the old hands and young hands walk for the good of man.
Let us be ready for the task ahead.
Let us go and plant the seeds.

My boy, the eyes of the suffering man await our hands.
Harden not your heart to fight for a just cause.
Today let us pledge our hands.
As I pray, Blessed Father, let compassion be our bedrock.

My boy, let us go with the light that others may see.
Let our hearts feed upon that which is good.
My boy, when this is done, let us run to the heart of the suffering man.
My boy, if I teach you well, let us go and do the Father's work.
My boy, the work must be done.
I know what I am doing.
Your young hands I ask of thee.

November 9, 2009

OUR FATHER

Our Father,
With these two praying hands,
In the name of the suffering man,
Let him rise up that others may see.

Father,
From my secret place,
The burden of the suffering man I lift to thee.
Open his eyes that he may see the light.
Open his heart to gladness.
Let the work of his mind be productive again.

Father,
Cut loose the bread of sorrows.
Remove the dirt off his frame.
Even though shame took a hold of him,
Help him to dream again.
When I looked at the aspiring youth,
A sense of loss took a hold of me.
His sense of reasoning I could not understand,
Yet I could not remove my ears.

November 9, 2009

LOOK, MY LOVE

Look, My Love,
I have seen the smoke, but I cannot feel the fire.
What fear is jumping at you?
Speak to me that I may adjust my steps.
Let not shame dress me down.
I do wish this madness would sleep.
Let the fire burn that I may run to thee.
Look, have I not eyes to see?
The brightness of the sun awakes my spirit.

November 9, 2009

A SONG OF PRAISE

Awake, my love.
Awake, my love.
Two little birds came to thee.
What sweet melodies they bring.
A song of love finding my ears.
Oh! Wind, take not their tender love away.
Let our hearts be full with such joy.
The sun with its light, allow mine eyes to roam the heavens.
My God, let me be thankful for such a beautiful morning.
When I look at nature,
Dancing trees find the rhythm of the winds.
Even though some sweet day I shall leave this land,
Let me give thanks to see the rising sun.
Oh! What a great day.
My dear, in the spirit of true love,
Let these two little birds do what they do best.
My dear, harden not your heart to spread the love.
In the name of humanity,
Come let us sing along.
Let us go to the heart of man and spread the wealth.
Blessed Father, today I call upon you.
Let a song of praise be upon our lips.

November 10, 2009

WHO SHALL I SEND?

My Boys,
Who shall I send to lead the way?
I am not worthy to make a selection.

Holy Father,
You have seen my plight.
Who should I send to lead the way?

My God,
Show me the way to leave my hands.
Could the first be the first, then the second follows?
Or could the second be the first, then the first follows?

Holy Father,
In secret I ask you to deliver my hands.

My Boys,
Let every man work to gain his wings.
Let the goodness of your hearts dictate your destinies.

My Boys,
May the teaching from this old man find your ears.
In the dead of night, I awake to prepare my hands.
In secret I allow my thoughts to shape my path.
To you, my boys, I dream on.
May peace and love be upon you both.

November 11, 2009

SLEEP

When a man cannot sleep,
Something heavy must be upon his mind.
My brothers and sisters,
Why worry over the things that you cannot control?
A man does need a place to rest.
A peaceful soul will find that joy to rest.
How can you sleep when your thoughts are at war?
A peaceful man will find sweet sleep.
Then allow dreams to roam.

November 11, 2009

PEACE AND PROSPERITY

Today I shall not be moved.
The rising sun I shall await.
Even though dark clouds blind my eyes,
The face of the sun I shall await.
The working of the mind I shall turn towards the heavens.

My God, my God, here I am.
At the mountain I stand crying out to thee.
For the good of man,
Bless this hand of mine.
Comforting words I ask of thee.
The weeping of the common man is upon the land.
What sorrows have I seen?
A land of plenty, yet man begging bread.
I have seen madness take a hold of man,
That I tremble in my boots.

Father, your people are in great need.
Darkness, my Lord, is upon the land.
Man running wild; what sorrows I have seen.

My God, let us see the light.
Let us find the will to live again.
Grand unto us mercy.
Today, today I cry to thee.
Let peace and prosperity be upon this land again.

November 11, 2009

GREAT SUN

Oh! Great sun, your face I have seen.
Let me follow your light.
The heart of the suffering man I cannot forget.
Let me warm my spirit that I may go on my journey.
There await the eyes of the suffering man.

Father, hold my hands that I may not fall.
Let me find the courage to stand firm.
A loving heart I beg of thee.

Father, if only I could find some good hands.
My day would be sweet.

November 11, 2009

MOURNING THE DEAD

On mourning the dead,
I have seen the living standing at attention.
A river of tears moving along.
Oh! What a gathering of the living souls.
Death, the stealer of man in full view.
My brothers and sisters, in honor of the dead,
Let the living continue the work.
Let us prepare ourselves for good deeds.
Tears or no tears,
The work must be done.
Let every man speak for himself.
The share of pain should not beat you down.
The rise and fall of man will continue.

November 11, 2009

MORAL PRINCIPLES

My Boys,
Let me speak.
When a man dedicates his life to certain moral principles,
The pain and pleasure of life will not dampen his spirit.
Earthly treasures will not fatten his heart.
A good man will feed upon good deeds.
The hands of the wicked will not excite his heart.
A fool will leap for joy, not knowing that death awaits him.

Today I shall look into myself.
Grandstanding I do not need.
On the shoulders of morality I stand.
Just as I am, I shall do the best I can.
The light of the eyes I shall use to enlarge my moral principles.

My Boys,
I will not leave my ideas hidden from your eyes.

My Boys,
The pleasure of life should not take away ones dignity.
Set your hearts upon doing good.

My Boys,
To serve mankind, follow the path of dignity.

November 11, 2009

OUR MINDS

My Boy,
Come to me.
Come let us find a place to reason.
On the subject of human sufferings I shall lend my years to you.

My Boy,
At this time we need some good hands.
Let us pray for the good of man.

My Boy,
I beg of you.
Let us apply our minds on doing good.
Even though you are young at heart,
There is no excuse for you not to follow the path of good.
I find myself taking my Father's hand.
He was a man with love, a man ready to serve.
Helping the poor was his passion.

Well, then, my boy,
You will see where I am coming from.
How can you escape such a path when you are my blood?
Come, then, let us unite to fight for a just cause.
Your young mind is of vital importance.

My Boy,
I will not allow my music to go to the grave.
Come dance with me.
Duty and only duty shall be my cry.
Let us go forth for the good of man.

November 11, 2009

THE ROARING LION

My Dear,
At last your eyes are mine.
No more dreams.
No more fasting.
No more weeping.
The time has come for rejoicing.
Sweeter than honey I have found.

My Friends,
Come and rejoice with me.
Let us pray for long life.
Oh! Mother, if you could see me now.
Proud as a peacock I stand.
When I remember your tender hands,
I shall do likewise.
Let true love be true love.
The roaring lion will stay within its gates.

November 12, 2009

I CANNOT HOLD MY HANDS

My Boy,
I cannot hold my hands.
True love took a hold of them.
How could I not bring them to you?
Words, my boy, fighting against each other just to be in line.
I shall try to be careful of my selections.
Sweet words, my boy, will be good for your tongue.
Even though young at heart,
Use your lips to move them for the good of man.

My Boy,
You have a job to be done.
I will not allow sleep to these eyes until I am able to lend you a hand.

My Boy,
Speaking of words,
Thcy are the food for you to feed upon.
Sweet words will take the heart.

My Boy,
A working mind can create wonders.

November 12, 2009

POOR MAN

Hidden from human wealth,
A poor soul looked to the heavens.
Alone and rejected by the rest of society,
A tired soul fended to stay alive.
Man and his troubled soul became a landmark.
The poor soul moved along.
From bins to bins, he searched for what was left.
The fall of man is in full view.
Only a sick man would turn to the dirt and he is not dead.
Are we not our brothers' keepers?

I cannot cry, but write.
I shall write with a heavy heart.
The tears I shall down inside.
If when he dies, tears should follow,
What shame would they heap upon this heart?

The mountain was his home.
The birds were his friends.
Let him become a part of nature.
My brother, may you find the hands of God.

Today I write in memory of the Bin Man.
May his soul rest in peace.

November 12, 2009

FACES I KNEW NOT

When I looked at the wicked hands of a mad man,
I saw faces I knew not dripping tears.
Yes, God, a nation is mourning.
A man their equal turned evil.
Shots upon shots spit from his weapon.
Mass destruction took a hold of his evil heart.

My God, what drove him to such rage?
In honor of our fallen brothers and sisters,
Let us call upon thee for a spirit of hope.
May the dead rest in peace.
May the shame upon this day open our hearts.
Father, let us find the courage to forgive.

November 12, 2009

IF I CANNOT LIVE

My Boy,
If I cannot live to teach you what is wrong from what is right,
What am I living for?
Well, then, I shall take time out to prepare myself.
On this day, with a peaceful mind,
I shall invoke the teaching of my parents.

My Boy,
Go to school and let us be proud.
Today those words become my food.

My Boy,
I shall urge you to do likewise.
Strive to gain that knowledge.
For the good of man,
Let fairness be your guide.
Walk with dignity to lend a hand.

My Boy,
Take a look into your ancestors' past.
What you find will give you courage to step into the future.
This old man is just a part of the picture.

My Boy,
If I had not followed the teaching of my parents,
Only God knows where I would be.

My Boy,
Seek and gain that wisdom from the elders.

November 12, 2009

THE BAG MAN

The Bag Man finds comfort within the mountain.
Day by day he strolls along.
What joy does he find from the garbage?
Laden with dead weight, he goes about his business.
Oh! Children of the Most High, make no mockery of this man.
He is one of God's children.
Who is he?
Why did he come?

Great God, you have seen the plight of this man.
Is he not in your book?
Where have all the good men gone?
Where are the Good Shepherds?

Father, what should I do?
Should I watch and pray or should I capture the plight of man?
Father, today I ask of thee, let me find the will to lend a hand.
What courage I need.
Awake, my spirit.
Awake, my spirit.
Power higher than I, here I am.
Dress me to lead.

November 12, 2009

LET US SING AGAIN

My Boy,
Come to me.
Come and let us sing again.
For the eyes of man,
Let us give of ourselves.
Today, today I ask of thee,
Come and let us sing again.

November 12, 2009

A SIGN OF PEACE

My Boy,
These are the words I shall feed upon.
"Blessed are the peace makers."
You came with love like a spring to a thirsty man.
From your love a new song is upon the lips of many.
Play Grandpa. Play Grandpa.
Nice Grandpa. Nice Grandpa.

My Boy,
By doing what is right,
There is a commitment towards peace.
You are the one to lead the way.
Sing on, my dear boy.
I will follow.
Let the gladness of your heart be a mirror to our eyes.
Peace and love I pray.

November 12, 2009

YOUR LOVE

My Boy,
With your love I now find pleasure in writing.
Your love came like sunshine to my soul.
I am a new man now.
The flow of words is like raindrops.
I shall now do what is right.
I shall stand up for the rights of love.
A peaceful heart will command respect.

My Boy,
I shall teach the children what is right from what is wrong.
You came to me with love.
It's now my duty to spread the love.

My Boy,
What the world needs is love.
Nation against nation, man against man, children against parents.
The will to love escapes the heart of the common man.

My Boy,
Hatred is like stain running among a body of people.
I am not pleased by the killings.
Man has gone mad, mad to the core.
When will man find the heart to be fair?
When will man find the heart to love again?

Blessed Father,
Your strong love and power I pray for this world.
Let the children play.
They shall lead the way.

My Boy,
Your love I shall speak thereof.

November 12, 2009

FREE

My Boy,
Your eyes set me free,
Free to look at the soul of humanity.
The power of love shall be my weapon of choice.
I shall fear no evil.
My poor mind cannot rest.
The burden of man rests within my chest.

Blessed Father,
Allow my burning desire to take root.
Allow my life to shine for the good of man.
Let my words be spice to the lips.
A seasoned soul I pray to find.
I have seen man in a state of unrest.
The burden of life took a hold of him.
Sadness took a hold of him.
The once cheerful man refused to smile again.

Blessed Father,
Turn him around that he may find the will to live again.
Let him enjoy the sweetness of life again.
Let him rise up to do that which is good.

Blessed Father,
In my free state of mind,
I took unto myself the burden of man.
Father, lead me that I may not fall.

November 13, 2009

BEFORE I WRITE

My Boy,
Before I write,
I set my heard upon peace.
Then put myself in a near trance.
Hidden words I then seek to find.
When I remember the suffering man,
I try to reason with a Higher Power.

My Boy,
To find good food, it takes time.
A man needs patience to wait upon his provider.
Great insight will be my calling.

Blessed Father,
At this moment, I am at a spot where I draw from my emotions.
Let true humanity fester my fingers.

My Boy,
I set myself to the tune of sweet music.
From the mountain I allow my soul to find peace.
To the East I allow my thoughts to feed upon that which is good.
I will allow no earthly treasure to dim my eyes.
The words, my boy, I meditate upon.
When I remember the eyes of the suffering man,
A part of me weeps.
Something must be done, my boy.
There must be an order to life.

My Boy,
Before I depart from this land,
I shall dedicate the working of this mind to the uplifting of man.

November 13, 2009

THE HEART

When a man prepares his heart to leave for his love,
He must be at peace within himself.
The gladness of the heart is laid to rest.

November 13, 2009

FIX THY FACE

My Dear,
Fix thy face that others may see.
Use your beauty for the good of man.
Find the will to love.
Seek and find the heart of the suffering man.

My Dear,
Boast not of your beauty.
Use your God-given gift to lift the spirit of these suffering men.

Blessed Father,
Hear my cry.
Send me some good hands.
By the mountain where I look beyond the sun,
Let the power fall upon me.
For the good of man,
Unit our hands.
As I warm my spirit,
Let me feed upon that which is good.

My Dear,
Take time out to do your Father's work.
Go and lift the spirit of the weary souls.

November 13, 2009

WELCOME

My Boy,
Let me invite you into my secret world.
Alone I focus on the uplifting of man.

Blessed Father,
Help me to learn to do good.
Good deeds will be upon my lips.
Mine eyes have seen the rise and fall of man.
When I listen to the fallen man,
What pity rests within me.
My heart becomes sick.

Father,
Let me find the courage to lend my hands.
Let hope be my dreams.
When this is done,
Help me to do that which is good.

November 13, 2009

MY BOY TANNER

The birth of a child,
An innocent soul came from the dark into the light.
What joy came along.
Oh! Mother, what happiness finds thee.
May you give praise where praise is due.
May you be thankful for a new life.

Holy Father,
You have seen the eyes of this innocent child.
May the angels keep watch.
Long life, my Lord, we pray.

November 13, 2009

THE CAPTAIN

My Boy,
If you find my thoughts coming to thee,
Remember I am the captain of this ship.
I have set my compass.
No storm will take away what is yours.
Alone I shall plot my course.
May God guide me through.
Let peace and love ride with me.

My Boy,
If I linger on,
Study ration will be my plan.
For the love of humanity,
I shall ask for your hands.
When I dance,
I will love to dance with you.
Mine eyes are getting dim.
Your young eyes I crave.
Blood to blood we shall unite.
Unity is strength, my boy.

My Boy,
It's me, the captain speaking.
If I cannot give of myself,
How could I ask of thee?
Look at my years.
I have seen a lot.

My Boy,
Learn from your elders.
What wealth to draw from.
May the gladness of this heart find favor with you.
Long live, my boy.
The work must be done.

November 13, 2009

A BURNING LAMP

My Dear,
If you would only allow the lamp to burn,
What light would I carry.
What gladness would be upon me.
What feast would be in the making.
Let the eyes that find thee be at peace to attend the gathering.

November 14, 2009

STAND AND SING

My Boy,
Stand and sing to the hearts of men.
Oh! My boy, what light I have seen.
This old man feeling young again.
I will give up my sleep to find words for thee.

My Boy,
From my fruits I shall feed thee.
Heavenly Father, you have seen this boy.
Lead him to the rock that is higher than me.
Where the old lion stands,
Let peace be upon the land.
Let the voice of the little one excite the heart.
Like a thirsty man seeking water,
So do I seeking thy sweet voice.
May the gladness of this heart find thee.
One love, my boy, may you shine for the good of man.

November 17, 2009

THE EYES OF MAN

When you look at God's heavens,
The formation of the clouds is a beauty to the eyes.
Such wonders are beyond the human mind.
Today I shall give praise to see the rising sun.
The eyes of the suffering man await my hands.
Father, you have seen my journey.
Let me set my compass.
As a humble man I shall go.
Who am I not to follow my calling?
The Father's work must be done.
My Lord, let me find the courage to stand firm.
Duty and only duty shall be my cry.
Father, help me to carry a loving heart.
The sorrows I have seen find the core of my soul.
Help me to bear the pain.
The return of man, I pray.
Help me to find comforting words.
Power higher than I,
Let me rise and rejoice to see another day.
The eyes of the suffering man await my hands.
Father, help me to enter His gates.

November 17, 2009

WHEN WILL MAN LEARN?

My God,
When will man leave his skin, then reach for his soul with a desire to love?

My God,
When will man leave his dust to a fertile spot?
Who is man to find fault of your creation?
Has he not eyes to see that the earth awaits what is left of him?

November 17, 2009

COME, MY BOY

My Boy,
The power of the human mind I will not underestimate.

My Boy,
Use your mind to create a climate of good.
Let your heart find the human spirit, a spirit that is filled with love.
Study the heart of good reasoning,
Then seek and find the soul of the children.

My Boy,
A child who feeds upon that which is good will produce that which
is good.
Well, then, let the old man speak.

My years are many.
The plight of man will never leave these eyes.
If I had not found the will to love,
My hands would be tight.

My Boy,
For the soul of humanity,
I shall let these hands loose.

My Boy,
The work must be done.
Who am I to run away from my calling?
Well, then, I shall press on.
Come, my boy, walk with me.
The eyes of the common man await our hands.

November 19, 2009

FIND THE WILL TO SERVE

My Dear,
Your eyes are like the stars.
Use them to excite the heart of the suffering man.
Today I call upon you.
For the good of man,
Harden not your heart.
Let the child from within come forth.

My Dear,
Let not cold sadness beat you down.
Find the will to love.
Find the will to serve.
Let your work speak for you.

November 19, 2009

WATCH AND PRAY

Run, my dear.
Run, my dear.
Run from the hands of the evil woman.
Let not her rage find thee.
Have you not eyes to see what took a hold of her?
Remember you are no match for those heavy hands.
Run, my dear, and find a place to hide.
A fool knows no boundaries.
My dear, watch and pray.

November 19, 2009

A TRUE TONGUE

My Boy,
When you find a tongue to be true,
There is no reason not to give of yourself.

My Boy,
A true tongue brings comfort to the heart.
A man in great need will lift his spirit to the movement of a true tongue.

My Boy,
When a tongue lifts sweet words,
It is like sweet music.
Music, my boy, helps to calm the soul.
Today my mind is bent on finding the rhythm I need.

My Boy,
One will find pleasure in the path of a sweet tongue.

My Boy,
Let me comfort myself by awaiting your tongue.
When I remember how you fed my spirit,
May the good Lord be with you.

November 19, 2009

FATHER OF ALL LOVE

My Boy,
As the sun finds my spirit,
So does your love.
Come, my boy, give unto me the fire I need.
From the cold I came to find your eyes.
What happiness greeted this heart.
Your sweet voice found my soul.

My Lord,
What gift have I received even though I fell?

My Boy,
I shall rise again.
I have seen the light through your eyes.

My Boy,
Today I am at the mountain.
Sweet music I shall feed to my soul.
No journey, no mountain shall entrap my thoughts.
The back of the minds I shall ride upon.
Raw emotions and all shall be with me.
Oh, love, take me to the heart of this boy!
No hands shall hold me down.
Sun, the warmer of man, here I am fingering my thoughts.
Love lifted my eyes toward the heavens.

Father of All Love,
From the mountain I cry to thee.
True love and only true love I shall preach.

November 20, 2009

DO YOU WONDER?

My Boy,
One love.
Let us join together and fight for the good of man.
My father and his father had done it.
Who are we not to follow in their footsteps?
Well, then, my boy,
Let me lead the way.
Let my years be your guide.
Let your ancestors' spirits find you.

My Boy,
Do not be afraid.
The Good Book said, "Blessed are the peacemakers."
The spirit of man needs to be tame.
I have seen man gone mad.
I said mad to the core.

My Boy,
I pray for your maturity.
Remember how you took comfort from your mother's breast.
Let these hands do likewise.
How I prepared them for you.
Night and day I prayed for your growth.
Hide not your eyes from sorrows.
Comforting words, my boy, should be your tool.

My Boy,
For my sake,
Be thankful for my hands.

November 20, 2009

FROM MY PLACE

My Boy,
When I prepared to write for thee,
Sweet words came to me.
In my place of study,
Silence allowed me to meditate upon the words.
Your picture and I facing each other's thoughts.
The young and the old bonding together.

My Boy,
This hand cannot rest.
The hands of time will not wait.
For the good of man,
The work must be done.
Why should I not reach for your young mind?
I have seen your spirit.
I have seen something good in you.
I have seen the eyes that look to thee.

My Boy,
Go to school and develop that mind of yours.
Seek that knowledge for the good of man.
Remember the common man.
If you cannot be humanlike, my boy,
You will find no sweetness.

November 20, 2009

223

WHERE IS THY LOVE?

My Dear,
Where is thy love?
Look at his closing eyes.
Death will come at any hour.
Let not his breath cease before peace.
I can only ask of thee to lighten your heart.
Let not ignorance take a hold of your heart.
It is better to love than feed upon hatred.
Let no shame be upon your bones.
Let him go in peace.
Be a just woman.
Fear not of the tongues.
Do what is right.
Then leave everything to a higher power.

My Dear,
I ask of thee,
Lend a hand to prepare his path.

November 20, 2009

NO ROOM FOR HATRED

Awake, my spirit.
Awake, my spirit.
It is time to go to the House of Suffering.
The face of man awaits my hands.
Who am I not to run to his eyes?

My Friends,
When sadness takes a hold of man,
There should be no room for hatred.
Like a man picking his strings,
A song of love should be upon your lips.
A loving heart should go forth.

Yes, My People,
Only love can heal the wounds.
Even though I walk through the dark,
The light, my people, I pray to find.
The return of man I dream of.

Blessed Father,
Help me to carry on.
Every man needs somebody.
May these hands do that which is good.

My People,
One love.
Remember the eyes watching you.

November 21, 2009

THE WATER OF LIFE

My Boy,
When I think of thee,
I cry out for God's mercy.
For your young mind I seek His guidance.
The water of life I pray that you will drink from.

My Boy,
Let us work together for the good of man.
Let the young and the old fight for a just cause.
Come to me and let us find a common ground.
In the mind of man I have seen a troubled mind.
Such sorrows reach the very soul.
His return needs a remedy.
Let us compose a song of love to charm his heart.

My Boy,
With your sweet voice I shall sing along.
If I had not seen the path of the Good Shepherds, my boy,
How could I focus?
Well, then, I shall speak no evil.
I shall feed thee upon true love.
What the world needs is love.

My Boy,
If I teach you well,
Let me be proud.
Go now, my boy, and do your Father's work.
Remember the work must be done.

November 22, 2009

THE HEART OF MAN

My Boy,
In the heart of man there is something good.
The tongue that sips from knowledge,
If used for the good of man will be a blessing.

My Boy,
I considered your love to be my joy.
What great heights I have reached.
Now I am hungry for knowledge.
The seat of higher learning I shall seek.
If I do not prepare myself,
How can I teach?
Well, then, my boy,
I shall drain from the great thinkers.
Then you and I can reason.
For the good of man,
We shall prepare our hearts.

November 22, 2009

WHAT AM I

My Boy,
What am I?
Why do I tell tears good night?
Sweet dreams I pray to find.
At the break of dawn,
I must go west.
Sometimes I wonder what cure I can find.
Man in his House of Pain dreams to be free.

November 22, 2009

THE BOY AND I

Searching my soul for the good of man,
Today I stand alone.
I shall allow good reason to dictate my path.
On the subject of man,
I shall keep watch and pray for a sound mind.
I have seen the best of minds fallen to madness.
Such sadness pulls out what pity I stored.
Man in a state of suffering needs some good hands.

My People,
Boast not of your standing.
Have you not eyes to see the fall of man?
We are all God's children.

My Lord, my Lord,
Why do I weep for the man I do not know?
Today I ask of thee,
Let me give of myself.
Let the boy and I do what is right.

November 23, 2009

THE MUSIC

My Dear,
Bring cool water to this thirsty man.
Roaming eyes will never rest.
Do not leave for I will fade away.
A heart that beats with such heaviness is not good.
The invitation of death will bring great sorrows.
Instruct me to do the right thing.
A man blinded by love cannot control his mind.
Well, then, my dear,
Listen to your heart.
Allow fairness to grace your heart.

My Dear,
Remember a good deed is what we preach.
If you can bring joy to the soul of a man,
Muster the courage to do what is right.

My Dear,
The music in my heart I shall take to thee.

November 23, 2009

WORK WITH THESE HANDS

Lamb of God,
You take away the sins of the world.
Have mercy upon your children.
Nation against nation.
War upon war all over this land.
Hatred spreading like brushfire.

My Lord, My Lord,
When will man learn to be his brother's keeper?
Where has all the love gone?
Where are the good men?
Where are the Good Shepherds?

Blessed Father,
I cannot control the tears.
What should I do?
Mine eyes are full.
The working of the mind cannot rest.
The suffering of the common man lay upon my chest.
Great protector of man,
Here I am.
Work with these hands.

November 23, 2009

MAY HE RISE

My Boy,
The sun came with such beauty that I am fixed to the East.

My Boy,
What can I do but dream of great things?
Sweet music finding the core of my soul.
Love, my boy,
Find a place to rest.
Yes, my boy, the sun in the sky brings forth my shadow.
Oh! Mountain from the sacred spot,
The power of love is upon me.
Let me find a song of love that I may dance with my shadow.
Eyes or no eyes,
The gladness of this heart will prevail.

My Boy,
It's a good thing I ran to the mountain.
My lost shadow would not have been found.
Oh! What a beautiful morning.
I have seen nature in its glory.
Man searching his soul to be at peace.
A humble man finding time to reason with his God.

True God,
Speak to me while I am in attendance.
In private I come to thee.
Let me bring forth the heart of this boy.
May he rise for the good of man.

November 23, 2009

WORDS

My Boy,
When I find wild words,
I put them in chains.
Then tame them for the heart of man.
I have seen man behaving like a wild beast.
Extra hands are called to put him in check.
Man with his violent nature can be controlled.
Remember he is nothing without his breath.
I have seen words bring man to tears.
In every man there is a soft spot.

My Boy,
If I can find words to cool him down,
I will not cease to bring out the good from within.

My Boy,
Day and night I work upon my craft.
May the eyes that find me be comforted.
Sweet words will allow the lips to move.

November 23, 2009

THE WILL TO SERVE

My Boy,
In the dead of night I refuse to give sleep to these eyes.
The work must be done.
The burden of man will never cease.

My Boy,
If you can reach one soul,
Your heart will find its gladness.

My Boy,
Peace with God will bring hope.
A peaceful man will find the time to serve.
Then await His blessings.

November 23, 2009

MY SANITY

My Boy,
I write to keep my sanity.
If I had not found my calling,
What would I do?

My Boy,
In a time like this,
Great sorrows are upon the land.
Man refuses to find the will to live.
The common man speaks nothing but hardship.

My God,
When will it end?
When will this nation prosper again?
When will love find the lips of its people?
Today I call upon thee.

Blessed Father,
Help us to carry the heavy burden.
As for me,
Let me be thankful.
I shall work upon my calling.

November 23, 2009

REACHING FOR YOU

My Boy,
If you find my hands reaching for you,
I have done my duty.
How could I not work for thee?
How could I not protect my eyes?
How could I not protect my hands?

My Boy,
In everything let me be thankful.

My Boy,
As I write to the sound of praises,
My mind is clear as crystal.
My thoughts will never leave thee.
Sweet songs are upon them.

My Boy,
I shall encourage you to seek knowledge.
From your knowledge scorn not the common man.
When I remember the words from my Father,
"Boy, they are poor. Feed them,"
How could I not honor such a man?

My Boy,
Remember you are my blood.
Let your ancestors find thee.

November 23, 2009

PROBLEMS

My Boy,
When everything seems to go wrong,
Do not get discouraged.
Lift up your heart to the Most High.
Pour out your troubles.
Then await His findings.

My Boy,
In a time of great uncertainty,
Pray on.
Leave everything in the hands of the Most High.
At this hour I shall meditate upon the words.

My Boy,
In all our needs,
Let the giver of all need dictate our paths.

Blessed Father,
Have mercy upon us.
Let your words be a comfort to our hearts.
Lead us to thy kingdom.
Then and there we shall worry no more.

Father,
Prevent us from going our own way.

November 23, 2009

AWAKE AT SUNRISE

Sweet Love,
Stay with me until mine eyes are closed.
Pray that my dreams will be sweet.
Pray that at sunrise I shall be awake.

November 23, 2009

HATERS

Oh! Love, let me rise with a full heart.
I have seen hatred jumping on the lips of men.
That I am afraid to speak.

My Lord, My Lord,
What shall I do?
Are they not your children?

Blessed Father,
Help me to find a cool head.
Dress me with courage that I may look at the eyes.
A praying hand I hope to see.

Father,
Let the haters return to love again.

November 23, 2009

A WEEPING HEART

My Boy,
I found my heart weeping for thee.
Oh! Journey dampen not my spirit!
Oh! Love lift me up.
Let the gladness of this heart find its destination.

Friends of Mine,
Take me to where I belong.
I shall teach the words to this boy.
A young mind that feeds upon that which is good will produce that which
is good.

My Lord,
You have seen the desire of this heart.
The eyes of the boy I pray to find.
I shall use this mind to cultivate comforting words.
A troubled man nccds to feed upon the words.

My Boy,
Forget not your calling.
Let me be filled with pride.
Put into practice what you learn.
I shall lay down my hands for you.

November 23, 2009

FINDING PEACE

My Boy,
When I feed upon sweet music,
What joy do I find?
Music, my boy, is good for the soul.
He should be at peace.
A man finding peace, his thoughts will be sweet.
For the love of humanity,
I cannot cultivate hatred.
Love, my boy, is the only way.
Let us work upon the children.
If you feed a child upon that which is good,
Such a child will produce that which is good.
A nation built upon love will keep its tears.
The roots of hatred will not find a fertile spot.

My Boy,
Cheer up from the dark.
There will be light.
All the world needs is love.
Let it not be said that you did not spread the words.
One love, my brothers.
One love, my sisters.
Peace be with you all.

November 24, 2009

ALLOW ME

My Dear,
Allow me to love thee.
Until the closing of the eyes,
The gladness of the heart shall be in words,
Where man may look thereupon.

November 24, 2009

SICKNESS

My Boy,
It's a very quiet morning,
A morning that sickness took hold of me.
I am not myself,
But will not play dead.
The work must go on.
My mind is fresh.
My hands are doing just fine.
Who am I not to follow my calling.
The burden of man will never cease.
A new day, a new case.

Blessed Father,
With this body,
Let me be thankful for the morning stars.
Even though lame,
I shall await the rising sun.
With praying hands I shall cry out to thee.

Blessed Father,
Remember your servant.
Touch me that I may be well again.
Remember the work must be done.
The eyes of the suffering man await my hands.

Awake, my spirit.
Awake, my spirit.
The work must be done.

November 24, 2009

THIRST

Oh, Love,
The written words I shall take to thee.
Let me drink from thy cup.
Look at my lips,
Thirst making a mockery of them.
Today I will allow my heart its desire.
Let your spirit be kind to me.
I am who I am.
At your gates I stand.
In the name of thirst,
I beg for your hands.
Let not my lips compete with the desert.

November 24, 2009

TAP INTO IT

My Boy,
Taming the wild best within a man takes time.
Courage, my boy, is a must.
Listening ears will create wonders.
Look for that one sign of weakness,
Then tap into it to bring out the child from within.
All men have some good within.

My Boy,
Focus on the task ahead.
Be true to thyself.
Put your God-given talent to work.
Reach for the weary soul.
Feed that soul upon that which is good.

My Boy,
Today I took time out to look at man.
I have seen man in a state of madness.
A mind that once caused heads to turn,
Now remains dormant to the ears.
Who am I not to seek pity?
Who am I not to pray for his return?
Who am I not to do the Father's work knowing that the work
must be done?

November 24, 2009

WHEN I WRITE

My Boy,
When I write a poem,
I reach for my soul.
Alone I focus upon my God.
If tears run like a river,
So be it.
The words I find I cannot leave.
Raw emotions or not,
I have to set my feelings free.
If I can bring joy to one soul,
My fingers would be rewarded.

My Boy,
This mind is bent on reaching the soul of humanity.
If I cannot appear humanlike,
Why finger these words?
Sweet words, my boy, I pray.
May I find a tongue to roll them for the good of man.
Oh! Great God,
You have seen the working of this mind.
Today I cry to thee.
For the good of man,
Let me pull from within that which is good.
Sweet words I pray.

November 24, 2009

THE VOICE OF A MOTHER

The voice of a mother,
Boy, you must read poems for me too.
How could I live without doing what is expected of me?
From the dead came the voice of my mother.

My Friends,
A dream that will never leave.

My Dear Mother,
What I ask of thee shall be done.
Your loving hands I will never forget.

November 24, 2009

LEAVE ME NOT

Oh! Love,
Leave me not to the hands of the evil one.
Take me to a place where I can hide.
High tides will not reach the mountain,
Even though burning bushes are on the rise.
My Love,
The rain might save my skin.

November 24, 2009

MY HEART CANNOT ESCAPE

My Boy,
My heart cannot escape the human sufferings.
Deep within my soul I search to find faithfulness.
Without faith, my boy, who am I?
Well, then, I shall muster the courage to share kind love.

Blessed Father,
Let me find your protection.
The heart of the common man I cannot predict,
Yet I try to give of myself.
Let me stand and face the rhythm.
How can I turn back when I have pledged my years?
What honor would I leave from my Father's teaching?
A man who has dedicated his whole life serving the poor,
Help me, Father, to follow his path.
When this is done,
May I find a place to rest.

November 24, 2009

AT YOUR MERCY

My Boy,
Swine flu or plain flu, I do not know.
But I am down with the flu.
I am now a broken man.
I wish I had my mother's hands.

My Boy,
A mother's love will heal all wounds.
Now I can only remember fond memories.
No one to rub my head.
No one with such tender hands.

My Boy,
Now I can only dream on.
Raw emotions are beyond my control.

My God, you have seen how weak I am.
Let me live that I may help others.

My Boy,
I shall find time to pray.

Blessed Father,
At this hour I come to thee.
Even though lame,
Touch me that I may be well again.
The spirit of my mother will never leave.
Let me find the courage to rise up.
For the love of humanity,
Let me find great healing to do my work.

Father,
The work must be done.
Your humble servant is at your mercy.

November 24, 2009

MY BOY, YOUR VOICE

My Boy,
While others find sweet sleep,
My head is raised picking words.
Alone I meditate upon the words.
Your picture keeps watch.
Your eyes urge me on.

My Boy,
The task ahead is not easy.
Who am I not to follow my dreams?
The words, my boy, should find the heart of man.
I will not allow sleep to beat me down.
I must keep the dream alive.
I must work upon my calling for the good of man.
Your spirit finds my spirit.
A new mind is born.
Words I knew not came like sweet music to my ears.
I shall play them for the heart of man.

My Boy,
With your sweet little voice,
Come sing with me.

November 24, 2009

THE DARKEST OF TIMES

My Boy,
In the darkest of times,
There is light.
Hold on my boy.
The Father giveth and the Father taketh.
Oh! Sun, the master of all lights,
From your heavenly beam I look beyond thee to find the ears of God.
True God,
Lead your people from the dark that they may see the light.
Lighten their feet that they may run with the light.

My Boy,
Today the sun is in its glory.
I and I finding bright eyes.
To the fallen man,
I pray that he may rise.
The fears that I have seen.
Father, help me to give of myself.

November 24, 2009

LIFE

My Boy,
In times of great difficulties,
One is allowed the time to reason.
Life with its many problems is a way of life.
Well, then, one should be prepared to fight on.
Go inside and draw from that inner child.
A child full of life will be on the move.
Fret not over the things that you cannot control.
Lean on your faith to pull you along.
Remember that there is a higher power.
In the time of great sorrows,
Lift up your burden to the great Father.

My People,
Watch and pray.
From the dark there will be light.
Await the light, my people.
Step by step,
Seek and find the hands of the Good Shepherds.

My Boy,
Today I took time out to search my soul.
The things I cannot control,
I will not let burden my mind.
There must be a way out.
Long life I pray.
What is to be,
Let it be.

November 24, 2009

A POET FINDING HIS SOUL

My Boy,
When a poet reaches the core of his soul,
Deep thinking takes a hold of him.
He will then call upon his spirit.
Heaven-bound his thoughts,
Seeking the ears of his God.
The burden of his heart will be exposed.
He will cry for words like a hungry man crying for food.
A poet in a state of atonement will find his conscience at peace.
A man finding peace will speak of love.
A loving world would be a gift to humanity.
Hatred would not find the oil to burn.
Man in his rush to acquire the power and glory will trade his soul
to adorn himself.
A poet will not hold his tongue in the face of injustice.
Death or no death,
He will speak his mind.

November 24, 2009

POETIC JUSTICE

My Boy,
I shall look at thee with the eyes of a poet,
A poet working his mind to spread love.

My Boy,
Love is the greatest gift.
What this world needs is love.
A loving people will please the heart of God.
Today hatred took a hold of man.
Man fighting for power and glory,
Not knowing that death awaits what is left of him.

My Boy,
Being a poet is not easy.
The burden of man will never leave.
The pain and suffering finds his soul.
A true poet will cry to his God for his hands.
Comforting words he will labor to find.
If you cannot carry a loving heart,
No poetic justice will find his hand.

November 25, 2009

GRANDPA'S LOVE

Grandpa's love is like water to a plant.
Young and tender his hands will set to work.
Praying that he will witness maturity.
He will be eager to share his years.
A man finding ripe age will not hesitate to shape the path of his blood.
Old eyes have seen the good and the bad.
Grandpa memories will not be put to waste.

November 27, 2009

HEALING HANDS

Sweet sleep, my beloved.
May sweet dreams be with thee.
May the guiding angels look over thee.
On your awake I shall be there.
I cannot leave now.
My mind is not well.
The suffering I have seen.
My knees will be in full use.

Holy Father,
Look at my beloved.
I cannot leave now.
Sickness took a hold of her.
Great healing I pray.
Power higher than I,
Your healing hands I pray.

November 27, 2009

THE STORM WILL PASS

My Dear,
Fret not thyself.
Everything will be alright.
The storm will pass.
Take everything to the Blessed Father.
Let your troubles be known.
Let loose your raw emotions.
Seek the hands of the Great Protector.
Do not be afraid of the dark.

My Dear,
The light will come.
From the light you shall trod upon a clear path.
May the hands of the Good Shepherds await thee.
Long life, my dear, I pray.
May peace be upon you.

November 27, 2009

I AM MYSELF

My Boy,
Today I am myself.
I am in a state of atonement.
The day after Thanksgiving I shall give thanks for what I received.
The eyes of the suffering men and women find many hands.
The spirit of togetherness was in the air.

My God,
I am thankful for the food we had.
Peace and love were all over the place.
Oh! What a day to be remembered.

November 27, 2009˙

THE HUMAN MIND

Oh! Heavenly Father,
At this hour I humble myself before thee.
What I have seen is more than I.
The human mind I cannot escape.
What pain and suffering confronted the eyes.
What sorrow eating away the heart.
Spirit of mine be still
The return of the minds I pray.

Father,
Here are your children crying out to thee.
Have mercy upon them.
Help their minds to feed upon the right food.
Let them return to the eyes of society.
Remove from their eyes the dark clouds.

Father,
Let them see the light.
Let them follow the path of the Good Shepherds.
Let joy return to their hearts.
Take away the sadness and allow gladness its seat.

Father,
Let hope be a beacon to peace and love.
Let society reclaim its people.
Let the bells of freedom find their ears.

November 28, 2009

YOUR LITTLE EYES, TANNER

My Dear Boy Tanner,
When I saw your little eyes,
The gladness of my heart filled my spirit.
Now, my dear boy, I shall speak to thee.
How proud I am to guide you along life's journey.

My Dear Boy,
Feed on.
May your future be bright.
It's alright with me.
A song of love I shall sing.
Sweet words I shall take to thee.
Oh! Love, take me to where I belong.
From this day I shall use my hands for thee.

Holy Father,
I beg of thee.
Let your hands be upon this boy.
Open your eyes that he may follow the light.
Let peace and love enter his heart.

My Dear Boy,
This old man has gone deep within his heart.
Words of comfort I shall leave for thee.
For the love of humanity, I beg of you.
Live and let others live.
Close not your eyes upon the suffering man.
Look at the path of your ancestors.
Go now, my dear boy, and do what is expected of you.
The work must be done.
Today, today I call upon you.

December 1, 2009

MORAL PRINCIPLES OF TRUE LOVE

My Boys,
If I cannot follow the moral principles of true love,
What teaching would I implement?
A loving heart will prepare that which is good.
My years I shall take into account.
Moderation, my boys, I shall follow.
Now let me take you inside of this mind.

True love will lift the spirit.
What this world needs is love.
I have seen man pump up with hatred that he foamed at the mouth.
When a man finds himself in such a state,
How can he reason?
What moral principle can he hold?

My Boys,
Run away from hatred.
Go and study the heart of your great grandfather.
He was a good man,
A man of love,
A man of peace.
The burden of the common man took him to his grave.

December 4, 2009

TANNER

My Boy, Tanner,
What shall I do?
I can see your eyes looking towards the future.

My Boy,
Let me watch and pray.

My Boy,
This body will be a servant to my conscience.

My Boy,
Your Grandpa pledged to fulfill a promise.
My love I shall not allow to fade.
I shall start by considering my raw emotions.
The power of love finds my soul.
Shame and guilt will not enter my thoughts.
You are my blood, and I shall stand to honor thee.
I shall keep an eye upon your growth.
What moral obligation rests upon me?
Moral feelings I will not allow to escape.

My Boy,
If I am not prepared to go the journey,
May this hand cease to write.
Well, then, let me work my knees.

Blessed Father,
In your name I present this little boy.

December 4, 2009

I SHALL WRITE TO THEE

My Dear Boy Tanner,
Today from my secret place I shall write to thee.
Even though you are too young to understand,
With the blessing of the Most High you will find my hands in the future.

My Boy,
For the good of man may you find time to serve.
Cover not your eyes from the suffering man.
Share the legacy from your ancestors.
Let their spirit find thee.
As I watch the hands of time,
Forget not this hand.

Boy,
Remember the work must be done.
Let me be proud.

December 4, 2009

THE CONDITION OF THE MIND

My Boys,
Words reflect the condition of the mind.
A fool will speak with a blind heart.
A humble man will speak from the goodness of his heart.

Boys,
From my secret place I cannot sleep.
The working of the mind is in full blast.
The collection of thoughts must be done.
The music from my heart I shall play.
A song of love I shall leave for the both of you.
My spirit will never leave you boys.
I shall give you both words of compassion.
If I teach you well,
Along life's journey do what is expected.
May your hearts be kind to the common man.

My Boys,
This world needs some good men.

My Boys,
This is my hour.
My heart I have lifted up to a higher power.
Your names I have submitted.

Boys,
Long life I pray.
Now that I have exposed myself,
I shall go to the mountain.

My Boys,
If I have not allowed reason to take its course,
Let me submit my heart for public viewing.

December 5, 2009

THE VOICE OF THE SUFFERING MAN

Awake, my spirit.
Awake, my spirit.
The voice of the suffering man will never leave my ears.

Blessed Father,
What shall I do?
Mine eyes cannot escape his fallen eyes.
Eyes like mine, yet he is far gone.

Power Higher Than I,
Let the eyes find their rhythm again.
Let the Good Shepherds come forth.
Praying hands will not leave.

Father,
Only time will tell.

December 9, 2009

BOYS, GO INTO THE WORLD

I think I will live to see a poem fitting the hearts of these two boys.
I will not rest this mind until the task is done.

My Lord, My Lord,
Sweet music finds my ears.
All praises to thee.
I shall humble myself, then put my thoughts together.
A poem of love I pray to find.

Oh, Young Minds,
Sweet words I shall leave within your eyes.
In harmony, my boys, fine-tune a song of love.

Boys,
For the love of humanity,
Use your minds to leave this world a better place.

My Boys,
With the blessing of the Most High,
All things are possible.

Boys,
Go to school and feed upon that knowledge.
Find the ears of the elders.
Draw from their wisdom.
When this is done,
Go into the world and let your voices be heard.

December 9, 2009

AT HOME

My Boys,
Today I am home,
Away from the eyes of the suffering man.
Two little birds came singing for a troubled heart.
The burden of man took a hold of me.

My Boys,
I shall listen to those sweet melodies.
The Father said if he provided for the birds,
Why should man worry?
I will not be unkind to this day.
Awake, my spirit.
Awake, my spirit.
Let I and I focus on the growth of the boys.
I cannot rest from writing.
The cry of the suffering man rings in my ears.

Boys,
I need some young hand.
Blessed Father,
Bless these two young minds.
For the good of man I pray for their guidance.
Little birds,
Sing on that I may find the rhythm for my song.

December 9, 2009

TIME TO EXPRESS LOVE

My Boys,
If I cannot find time to express my love,
What am I living for?
What legacy would I leave?
Well, then, let me speak.
I shall allow the child from within to direct my tone.
True love came to me like two little birds.
Oh! Wondering eyes be still.
Do not be afraid.
It is I and I,
A man from another land who came to this land for a purpose.
Love and only true love I shall preach.
There is no time for hatred.
Oh! Young souls feed upon that which is good.
Let your light shine for the good of man.
Forget not the hands of the Good Shepherds.

Boys,
Remember the work must be done.
Early I rise to do what I love to do.
The power of the words, my boys, should be your tool.

My Boys,
Stay with me.
I shall lead the way.
Let true minds follow the path of good.
Let true love be true love.

December 9, 2009

263

I CANNOT TURN BACK

My Boys,
Today I am in the heart of the suffering man.
Year by year I linger on.
Now I cannot turn back.
My mind is bent on doing good.
The teaching of my Father rests upon me.
"Boy, you know that they are poor."
"Somebody has to take care of them."
Those words will never leave.
Well, then, my boys, for the good of man,
Let us unite to fight for a just cause.
I have dedicated my youth working to uplift the spirit of man.
Now that I am in my prime,
The time is right for me to share the legacy.

Boys,
I pray that I will find your ears.
Let your ancestors be proud.

My Boys,
If I teach you well,
Let my name be upon your lips.

Holy Father,
You have seen this heart.
Let my work speak for me.
Bless the hearts of these two boys.
Let them find the courage to do that which is good.

December 9, 2009

THE NEWS

My Boys,
I awake to the news.
Nation against nation.
War upon the land.
While they fight for power and glory,
Murder and starvation parades their ugly faces.
When will man learn to be his brother's keeper?
When will love take a hold of hatred?
What lesson is learned from the past?
When will man resort to good reasoning?

My Lord, My Lord,
When will the suffering end?
When will man find the will to love?

December 9, 2009

CULTIVATE LOVE

My Boys,
To cultivate love,
It must be your business.
In the dead of night,
I allow love to take its roots.
I will not allow sleep to find a heavy heart.

December 11, 2009

LOOKING AT MAN

My Dear Love,
On this night I look at man with pity.
What sorrows I have seen.
What pain I have seen.
With keen eyes I stand alert.
The working of the mind cannot find peace.
My God, is he not in your book?
What should I do?

Father,
Let me find comforting words.
Let me find the right tone of voice.
Let mine eyes be firm.

Power of the Most High,
Forget not this man.
Even though he falls,
Let him return to his rightful mind.
Let him find the will to be good again.

Father,
On this night I beg of thee,
Forget not your children.
May the suffering man find his true calling.
Let him see the light that he may follow.

My Dear Love,
I shall speak no evil.
Let my raw emotions be who I am.

December 12, 2009

NO TEARS SHALL BE SAVED

My Dear,
When I write for thee,
No tears shall be saved.
The trueness of the heart shall come to thee.
Love in its splendor shall find thy face,
A face that I will remember.

My Dear,
A time to cry,
A time to love,
Let true love find its course.

December 12, 2009

A JOYFUL SOUL

My Boy,
A joyful soul will find peace.
I have seen man's lips jumping like frogs.
Hatred took a hold of him.

My Boy,
Stay away from the street of hatred.
At this hour I am putting my years into your young mind.
Mine eyes have seen the fire set by hatred.
My message to you is listen to your own goodness.
Take the light to the heart of the suffering man.
Behind the smug face, let the child from within come forth.
Try your best to be a Good Shepherd.
I have seen that love in you.

My Boy,
If I do not share my years with you, how can I go in peace?
In the dead of night I awaken.
Your face will never leave.
The hands of time I keep watch.
The working of the mind I set upon thee.
This is the life of a poet.
How can I rest

December 13, 2009

A DAY OF REST

My Boy,
Today is a day of rest, yet I cannot rest.
The eyes of the suffering man will not leave.
The face of sadness became a mirror to the eyes.
Now that I have time to think,
I shall call upon the Blessed Father for guidance.

My God,
Here I am facing noon.
No food shall enter this mouth.
Eastbound I shall look to thee.
Man and his fallen eyes are in great need.

Oh! Great One,
The lying of your hands is in need.
My God, every man is special to you.
I, the holder of this pen, pledge this hand for the good of man.
What dignity do I crave?
The little things that I can do.
For the good of man,
With clean hands here I am.

My Boy,
The work must be done.

December 14, 2009

IN THIS MOMENT

My Boy,
In this moment of silence,
I shall take the time to shape my thoughts.
The wisdom of life I shall share with you.

My Boy,
Live and let others live.
If you witness a fallen man,
Poke no fun at him.
We know not our end.
Today for me, tomorrow for you.
Well, then, my boy,
Let your light shine.
For the good of man,
I beg of you, lend a helping hand.
Boast not of your standing.
Humility, my boy, is the way to go.
A humble man will find time to love.
A humble man will know his hands.
This world needs some loving hands.

My Boy,
Stand with me.
Let us fight for a just cause.
The dignity of humanity I pray.

December 14, 2009

THE SPIRIT OF TRUE LOVE

My Boy, Tanner,
The mind is there.
The spirit of true love is riding high.
The eyes of a people are upon us.
Let them see what is true love.
Let man and boy display the true meaning of strong love,
A love that came from the purity of the heart.

My Boy,
What the world needs is love.
Let us go forth and spread the wealth.
Let us use our voices to sing for a change.
In harmony we shall stand upon that stage,
Man and boy working to make this world a better place.
Oh! Love, take us to the hearts of the weary souls.

Blessed Father,
Help us to make a nation unite in the spirit of true love.
Wipe away the stain of death from this land.
Let its people find the will to love again.

Blessed Father,
Today I run to the mountain.
My heart I present to thee.
Let the power of love rescue your people.

Father,
From the mountain I cry to thee.
Let a song of love find our lips.

December 14, 2009

A MIND WITH HATRED

My Boy,
When a man uses his mind to cultivate hatred,
Allow the power of love to find his conscience.
Grand peace is what is right.
The glory of a peacemaker shall be a blessing to the heart.
A man who walks in peace will attract many eyes.

Oh! Great Ruler of the Universe,
You have seen man and his evil heart.
A whole nation crying out to thee.
Its people beaten down with great sorrows.
The blood of death all over the land.
Oh! What a confusing man to allow hatred to drive him into a
state of madness.
My God, my God, when will it end?

Blessed Father,
Come to our rescue.
Let the people find the will to love again.

December 14, 2009

PRIDE

My Boy,
I shall speak of thee with pride.
What precious gift have I received.
I shall not hide my love for thee.
You came with fresh soil for the old roots,
Knowing that you are a branch striving for maturity.

My Boy,
You have done your best.
The rest will be history.
A child with the same blood will find its fountain,
Knowing that things will turn out for the best.

My Boy,
True love will serve as a guide to action.
What courage finds your young mind?

December 14, 2009

I AM MYSELF

My Boy,
With the working of this hand,
I am myself.

Blessed Father,
Help me to do the work.
Let me take pride in shaping my path.
I am a man with love.
I believe in love.
True love will bring a loving heart.
A loving heart will bring happiness to others.
What this world needs is love.

December 14, 2009

WASTE NOT YOUR MIND

My Boy,
Waste not your mind upon petty things.
Dream of great things.
Aim your heart upon a higher calling.
You have a mind of your own.
The whole world is watching you.

My Boy,
Use your mind to focus on the uplifting of man.
Follow the path of the great thinkers.
Draw from their knowledge,
Then set your compass.
Today I am in a state of deep thinking.
The working of the mind I shall use for the good of man.
True peace rests upon me.

My Boy,
Come with me that we may sing along.
I shall await your young hands.
Your youth is of vital importance.
Let the years of the old man be your guide.

My Boy,
Even though down on my knees,
A chance will come.
The power of the Most High will find a way.

My Boy,
Let us find the courage to serve.
Stand by me and I shall lead the way.

December 14, 2009

WHERE DO YOU WANT ME?

My Boy,
Where do you want me to sing?
I am at your service.
A song of love took a hold of me.
You and I shall call upon the heart of man.

Blessed Father,
Here I am.
Let me find the courage to use this voice of mine.
Let the boy and I harmonize for the heart of man.
Peace and only peace we crave.

December 14, 2009

THE CURSE OF HATRED

My God,
When will man find time to love?
The curse of hatred took a hold of his soul.
Strong winds I beg of thee.
The foundation of man needs to be cracked.
Man needs to find himself,
Trying to keep his balance.
In the act of doing,
He will find time to focus.

December 14, 2009

THE BOYS

My Boys,
To keep my mind in shape,
I feed upon the words.
That my tongue will be in shape.
A loose tongue only brings disgrace.

December 14, 2009

NOTHING BUT PEACE

My Friends,
I come to you with peace.
Let us offer the peace sign.
What this world needs is peace.

My Friends,
Here I am.
Take me as I am.
Noting but peace I pray.

December 14, 2009

PEACE

My People,
Come, let us drink from the peace cup.
Let us champion for a good cause.
Let us find unity among our people.
The face of hatred is spreading all over the land.
Let us fight for a just cause.
Where there is hatred,
Let peace find its course.

My People,
Unity is strength.
Let us bond together and fight.
Peace and only peace shall be our cry.

December 14, 2009

WEST BOUND

My Boy,
Early I rise to face the task ahead.
The eyes of the common man await my hands.
West bound I must go.
Upon a hill I must stay.
The House of Suffering stands firm.
The plight of man is in full view.
Wandering feet are on parade.
Man is in a state of suffering reaching for some good hands.

My Boy,
The sun will allow my spirit to find its rhythm.
West bound I must go.
The eyes of the common man await my hands.

December 14, 2009

SHAKE UP THIS PLACE

My Dear,
When a man finds love,
The gladness of his heart lifts his spirit.
A man in love will give of himself.

My Dear,
This world is starving for love.
Hatred is too much for the heart of the people.
The ugly face of war drives man mad.
Madness rises like yeast.

My Lord,
How long shall hatred destroy your people?
Where are the pace signs?
Man dresses in rage letting loose upon the land.
Leaving the stains of death that rob others of their tears.

My Lord, My Lord,
How long shall the wicked run loose?
Where are the birds of peace?
Where have all the lovers gone?

Blessed Father,
I come to you this night.
Shake up this place that man may learn to love again.
A loving people will find a song of love.
Then offer praises to thee.

December 15, 2009

A LOVE MADE IN HEAVEN

My Boy,
I am just a boy in an old man's body.
Come, let us play.
A song of love will be just right.
Even though ripe age finds me,
I am doing just fine.

My Friends,
Come and see with your two eyes,
A love made in heaven.

December 15, 2009

WATCH YOUR HANDS

My Boy,
Let not your hands be against your brothers and sisters.
Use them to do that which is good.
As for me,
With this hand I shall write for thee.
I will allow these fingers to dictate my path,
A path that I will mark for thee.
Let me use this hand to draw from my soul words of comfort.

My Boy,
True love will define my thinking.
Let our minds be in tune.

December 15, 2009

SEASON

My Boy,
In this cold I commit my hands.
Pain or no pain,
The work must be done.
As I await the sun,
Let me set my mind upon that which is good.
The festive season is upon us.
Let me pray.

Blessed Father,
Remember the rich and the poor.
May the strong lend a helping hand.

Father, those with nothing,
May the Good Shepherds find their eyes.

Father,
In this time of great stress,
Let joy be upon the hearts.

December 18, 2009

SPEAK TO ME

My Dear,
Should I stop my love from feeding upon thee,
Or should I allow it to fatten for thee?
May the working of the eyes speak to me.

My Dear,
Speak to me that I may protect this heart.
Heaving breathing is not good for its use.
A happy man will bring out his music.
A song of love will be upon his tongue.
When a man allows his emotions to overflow,
He is ready to take a step forward.

December 18, 2009

THE TASK MASTER

My Boy,
Do not allow the task masters victory.
As I pray,
Go to the House of God.
Unity, my boy, I beg of you.
If it is God's will,
Your young eyes will be my old eyes.

My Boy,
The tradition of good hands will never end.
Face to face we shall stand.

Blessed Father,
Open your eyes to true love.

Oh! Children of the Most High,
Prepare thy hands.

December 18, 2009

I WILL

My Dear,
If I find your tongue to be true,
I will gladly give of myself.
A true tongue is good for the spirit.
Today I rise to honor thee.
Let the working of our minds find a common ground.

Eyes like mine.
Face like mine.
Let good reason find our lips.
Let peace and love be upon us.

My Dear,
A true tongue is all I ask of thee.

December 19, 2009

DEEP THINKING

My Boys,
Today I am in the mood of deep thinking.
If you should find my hands on this day,
My thoughts are with you both.
The working of the mind I allow to focus on true love.
A man finding love will find sweet words.
A loving heart will feed upon that which is good.
Even though man to man is unjust,
I shall continue on my journey.
Rich or poor,
I care not.
The work must be done.
I shall leave this world a better place.

December 19, 2009

GIVE LOVE A CHANCE

When a man cannot find happiness,
How can he love?
A man needs to find a loving heart.
Then the spirit of happiness will be upon him.

My Friends,
A clean heart will attract that which is good.
Well, then, my friends,
Go for it.
Let the spirit of true love dwell within thee.
Find its rhythm.
Then sing along.
A happy man will sing like a free bird,
Attracting the eyes of others.
Life is short.
Give love a chance.
Then allow happiness to set fire to your feet.

December 19, 2009

HOW FRAIL I AM

My Dear,
My wish arises with my love.
Your laughter feeds my heart.
Your sleep I pray upon.

My Dear,
I hope your arrival will be bright.
Dreams, my love, tainted by night.
How frail I am to thy love.
Come to me, my dear, that I may sing for thee.

December 20, 2009

A LOOK AT HUMANITY

A poet in a state of deep thinking will allow his mind to
look at humanity.
He will find words to confront man.
A poet cannot hide his eyes.
He will allow his conscience to speak for him.
A poet will not rest until the work is done.
I don't know why a poet took unto himself the burden of man.
Only God knows his reward.

December 20, 2009

SET HIM FREE

My Dear,
Set him free.
How he begged to be loved.

My Dear,
Where do you carry your heart?
Day by day I prayed for the poor soul.
Let him live that he may fulfill his dreams.
I have seen where he put his heart into your very hands.
What happiness I have seen upon his face.

My Dear,
I beg of you.
Set him free for the world to see.
I have seen something good in him.
Turn not away his probing eyes.
You know not his breeding.
A bird in the hands is better than many in the threes.

My Dear,
I can only ask of thee to show compassion.

December 21, 2009

A WITNESS

The boy and his love,
Even though young at heart,
His young mind directs his tender heart.
A path of true love finds its calling.
Old eyes cannot stand their ground.
True love, the mover of the spirit, is what the world needs.
A boy with his youthfulness reaching the heart of man.
The Good Book said, "A child shall lead the way."
Today I am a witness.

December 21, 2009

QUEENIE

My Dear Queenie,
We salute you for a job well done.
Your hands were freed.
Your attitude touched by the hands of God.

My Dear,
You have set an example for us to follow.
May the good God take you on your next phase.
What love you shared with us.
You are one of a kind.
Easy on your tongue.
You will be in our prayers.

Blessed Father,
Let her enjoy the fruits of her labor.
A job well done, my dear.
The angels must be singing a song of praise.

My Dear,
Your work will speak for you.
Let us rise to honor thee.
Farewell, my dear.
Farewell, my dear.
Let your work speak for you.

December 21, 2009

A TIME TO LOVE

Deep love will flow like a spring.
Drink, my dear.
Fatten your heart.
Let it be a time to love.

December 22, 2009

WE SHALL MEET

Here lies my beloved.
My one and only true love.
No more eyes for me to follow.
No more tears for me to wipe.
How can I live without you?
What joy will I find?
What songs will I sing?

My Dear,
It will not be long before I come after thee.
I find no purpose standing alone.
This heart is now strange to thy clothing.
Heaven-bound, my dear,
I pray we shall meet again.

December 22, 2009

THE HEART OF A MAN

A man that follows his heart to do good will not trod upon an easy road.
He should be careful of the hands of evil.
If he cannot cultivate a loving heart,
What joy will he find?
The burden of the suffering man will awake his spirit.
One needs to find deep faith.
If he cannot carry the love for humanity,
What drive will he find?
A good man will pledge his service.
His eyes will be set upon the prize.
Fitted wings will be his dream.
A good man will not soil his hands.

Father,
Where there is hatred,
Let there be love.
A good man will find the passion to leave his hands.
Then allow history to take its course.

December 24, 2009

I SHALL WEEP NO MORE

Oh! Love,
Today I shall meditate upon the sun.
No matter where you are at this moment in time,
My spirit will come after thee.
Long life I pray.
Love and only love I shall feed upon.
When a man finds peace,
His thoughts will be sweet.
His mind will be fresh.

My Dear,
I shall use these hands to search for thee.
Cold or no cold,
I shall continue.

Great Master of the Universe,
You have seen the eyes watching me.
Little birds at my rescue,
What sweet songs they bring.
A song of love graces my ears.

Oh! Love,
Come forth and sing with me.
Let the mountain be our meeting place.
Let the sun be our witness.
Then and there I shall weep no more.

December 24, 2009

FRIENDS OF MINE

My Friends,
When I write,
I write to pull the imagination.
As for me,
I find a state of near perfect peace.
Such a state will allow me to be humanlike.
The dignity of humanity finds my soul.
I came to this world finding two loving parents.
From their teachings I shall do what is expected of me.

My Friends,
Live and let others live.
Hide not your face from the fallen man.
Remember we are all God's children.
Seek and find the path of the Good Shepherds.

My Friends,
Try to leave this world a better place.

December 24, 2009

TIME WILL TELL

My Boy,
My Father had loved his Grandfather.
That he received his legacy.
You are doing what is right.
It runs in the family.
Keep on doing what you're doing.
Time will tell what is true love.

December 24, 2009

DEEP PEACE

My Boy,
I did not ask for happiness.
It came to me.

My Boy,
You came to this world for a purpose.
Not in my wildest dream did I think of the unknown.

December 24, 2009

THE CONSCIENCE OF A MAN

In the dead of night,
I call upon my spirit to be bold.
The plight of human dignity is like sores to the eyes.
How long, my Lord...how long, my Lord shall the suffering man seek pity?
Oh! What a shame upon the land.
Who is he?
What smell have I encountered?
Where are the good hands?
A fallen man stepping out in rags.
What fear I have seen.
Where are the virtues of the strong?
The children made a mockery of what is left of him.
Where are the hands of the Good Shepherds?
How long shall I moan.
How long shall I drown myself in tears?

Great God,
Is he not in your book?
Every many deserves sympathy in a state of crisis.
Now that I have reported accurately what I have seen,
May my conscience be at peace.

December 24, 2009

DEEP WITHIN MY HEART

Sun, the warmer of man,
Here I am.
Shine upon me.
Strong winds moving along the trees.
My God, what a beautiful morning.
Oh! Mountain, from your sacred spot,
The East I commit my spirit.
What peace I find.
Blessed Father, for the good of man,
Here I am.
Let me find sweet words to comfort his troubled heart.
Alone I stand crying out to thee.
Deep within my heart,
I allowed this mind to feed upon that which is good.

Blessed Father, help me to focus on the beautification of man.
I have seen madness take hold of man.
Man in a state of madness needs some good hands.
Father, today I come to thee a broken man.
As I find the sun,
Let me find thy ears.
For the good of man,
Answer me.
Let my work speak for me.

December 24, 2009

DRESSED IN HATRED

When I look at man dressed in hatred,
I pity the fool.
No time to love.
No time to reason.
No time to sing.
No time to calm his heart.
Why should a man choose to be on the wrong side of history?

December 24, 2009

WHEN A MAN IS DOWN

What happens to a man when he is down?
A low spirit will linger on.
Great dreams will be of the past.
Courage, my dear friends, will be the only hope.
A man should keep his eyes upon the prize.
Find his knees and keep hope alive.
While there is life, there is hope.
I have seen man rise from rags to riches.

My Friends,
Reach for that child within.
Let the child find its true rhythm.

December 24, 2009

WORKING FINGERS

My Boys,
When I am dead,
Leave me no tears.
Seek and find the words,
Then feed upon them.
I have lived a long life,
A life that I have dedicated to the suffering man.

Boys,
In remembrance of me,
Let my work speak for me.
I have done my best.
If history should find me,
Go to the heart of the children.
Let the words be their food.
If you feed a child upon that which is good,
Such a child will produce that which is good.
Then the working of my fingers would be a blessing.

December 25, 2009

THE HOUSE OF KNOWLEDGE

My Boys,
When you receive my hands,
You will be getting knowledge from the heart.

Boys,
Study the words, then feed upon them.
Invest yourself in learning.

Boys,
Knowledge is power.
For the good of man,
Do the right thing.
Help the weak that they may become strong.
The suffering man will need a helping hand.

My Boys,
The continuation of peace must go on.

My Boys,
True love will teach us the heart of good reason.
In the dead of night,
These words burn into my brain.
When will man find the will to love?
Nation against nation.
War upon war all over the land.
Madness took a hold of man.

My Boys,
There will be no peace without taking action.
The work must be done.
Find the courage to serve.
Go to the House of Knowledge,
Then plot a course to go on your mission.

December 25, 2009

THIS IS MY HAND

My Friends,
This is my hand.
What you see is what you get.
Take a good look at its working.
The burden of man took a hold of it.
If my fingers could talk,
The pain and pleasure would be a lesson.

My Friends,
Love cannot be kept by hatred.
At peace I dream of a loving heart.
How sweet it is to be in love.
A loving face is what the world needs.

December 25, 2009

SOMETHING MUST BE DONE

When a man finds his calling in life,
His passion will be like a burning fire—no time for cooling.
Every man should follow his dreams.
As for me, I cannot hold my emotions.
The voice of the common man will not allow me to sleep.
Something must be done.
Blessed Father,
Send me some good hands.

December 25, 2009

LISTEN TO YOUR CONSCIENCE

My Boys,
If I function like a well-oiled machine,
I have gone to the rock that is higher than I.

My Boys,
Duty and only duty shall be my cry.
For the good of man,
These hands cannot rest.
The burden of the suffering man will not leave.
Forgive me of my daily cry.
The pain and pleasure goes hand in hand.
When a man allows his conscience to drive his path,
There will be no turning back.
The singing of the angels will take him along.
Heave-bound will be his only cry.
A pure heart will be his trademark.
In the name of humanity,
The work must be done.

My Boys,
Listen to your conscience.

December 25, 2009

THE WORDS OF A GRANDFATHER

My Boy,
A grandfather is a man who has seen life,
A man who has gained a wealth of knowledge.
Love for the grandchildren will never cease.
The continuation of the family brings great pride.
The youthfulness of the children is bright lights to his eyes.
As for me,
I am one proud old man.
How I remember my father's love for his grandchildren.

My Boys,
I am just following his footsteps.
Love, my boys, is the foundation of a family.
Who am I to stray from my father's teaching?
To you, my boys, I lift up my love.
It's me, not your father.
It's me, your grandfather.

Boys,
Let your ancestors be proud.

December 25, 2009

PURSUIT OF PEACE

My Boy,
The pursuit of peace is a must.
Without a bundle of love,
The task cannot be achieved.
Where there is hatred,
Allow love to take its root.
Courage, my boy, is a must.
Seek to find that tender spot.
Then work upon it.

December 25, 2009

IN PRAYERS

My Boy,
When I call for thee in prayers,
The burden of man I take along,
Hoping that my hands will direct you along life's journey.
The rivers of tears, I pray, will leave its mark.

My Boy,
Allow no man to take you along the wrong road.
You have a mind of your own.
Pray for daily guidance.
Remember that you are the first.
All eyes are upon you.

As for me,
I have seen something good in you.
When I give up my hands,
I expect that you will carry the light.
Find that burning desire to do what is expected of you.
By all means,
Find the heart of the children.

My Boy,
If I teach you well,
Remember to share the legacy.
As you watch the hands of time,
Forget not my hands.

December 25, 2009

MY BOY, COME TO ME

My Boy,
Come to me.
Let us reason man to man.
Even though young at heart,
For the good of man,
Let us fight for a just cause.
The cry of the suffering man cannot be ignored.
Let us find the will to serve.

My Boy,
If I teach you well,
Harden not your heart towards humanity.
I beg of you,
Be humanlike.
Use your charm to reach the suffering man.
Fold not your hands.
Use them for the good of man.

My Boy,
What we need is love.
With true love there will be no need for war.
We must fight together to leave this world a better place.

My Boy,
Use your sweet voice to carry a song of love.
I and I shall sing along.

My Boy,
Remember the work must be done.
Come, let us fight for a just cause.
Let good reason be our weapon of choice.

December 25, 2009

CHRISTMAS

My God,
On this day I pray for those who cannot give.
Touch their spirits that they will dream on.
Let not the burden of suffering dampen their spirits.
While there is life, there is hope.

My Brothers and Sisters,
Dream on.
Find your knees,
Then cry out.
The Great Master will lead the way.
Everything has its season.
The rain came.
The sun came.
Your day will come too.

My Brothers and Sisters,
Look beyond the sun,
Then wish upon the desires of the heart.
By the power of the Great God,
A dream will come through.
Today, my brothers and sisters,
Let peace and love be upon you.
Fret not thyself.
Beyond the dark clouds there is light.

Oh! Great Sun,
As I look upon your face,
Your light I shall follow.

December 25, 2009

MERRY CHRISTMAS TRISTAN

My Boy,
If I teach you from a young age,
By the grace of God,
You will grow in the way of a godly man,
A man of peace and love.

My Boy,
Today is Christmas morning.
Early as I rise,
Mine eyes set to the east.
The ears of God I pray to find.
Peace and love I bring to you, my boy.
For the good of man,
I pray for you.
You are a gift from God to me.
What sweetness I find in you.
What love I received.
The virtues of a good man will find a receiving heart.

My Boy,
As I follow the hands of time,
My hands reach for thee.
Merry Christmas and may wisdom be upon thee.

December 25, 2009

ONE LOVE

Awake, my spirit.
Awake, my spirit.
The voice of a boy is calling.
No cold, no heat shall dampen my spirit.
The call must be addressed.
The working of the mind must take its course.
One love and only one love shall be my cry.

December 25, 2009

WORDS TO FEED UPON

My Boy,
Words to feed upon.
Let your young heart be in tune with the suffering man.
Stay away from pride.

My Boy,
Be humanlike.
Live and let others live.
If you see man and he is hungry,
Feed him.
Heap no shame upon him.

My Boy,
A good deed is expected of you.
On this day I come to you from the heart.
The uplifting of man is a must.

My Boy,
The work must be done.
You are blessed with your youthfulness.
Corrupt not its path.
Let your young hands plant good seeds.

My Boy,
You will be the captain of your own ship.
Take time out to set your compass.
Set sail to find the heart of man.
Today I find the sun.
Beyond the sun I pray for thee.
Great wisdom I wish for thee.
Oh! Master of the Universe,
Let this boy shine for the good of man.
Today, today I call upon thee.

December 25, 2009

YOUNG EYES

My Friends,
A child will be the eyes of the elders.
What precious gift has been handed to man.
Well, then, my people,
Lay not your hands upon the children.

My Friends,
A child carries a body of innocence,
Young in heart and in need of guidance.
True love, my friends, is the most important thing.
If you feed a child upon that which is good,
What bright eyes will see you.
Remember when the time is right,
They will be your new eyes.

My People,
In good times remember the growth of the children.
Nothing but strong love should be your cry.
Today I am looking at a picture of my young eyes.

Let me pray.
Blessed Father,
Let me find the will to love these young eyes.
Help me to feed this child upon that which is good.

December 28, 2009

IF I COULD ONLY SEE YOU NOW

My Boy,
If I could only see you now.
A song of love would find my ears.
Here I am looking at a dancing tree.
From the mountain I shall send my love to thee.

Oh! Great Winds,
Let my love ride upon thee.
Oh! Take me to the heart of this boy.
No mountain, no valley shall hold me down.
The spirit of love shall remove all fear.

My Boy,
Whatever it takes,
I and I shall be there.
Awake, my spirit.
Awake, my spirit.
Eastbound the voice of the boy calls.
Who am I not to answer the cry.
When a man finds love,
The gladness of his heart sets his feet on fire.
Deep within the soul,
His tears will put out the fire.

Oh! Great Mountain,
From your sacred spot,
The hands of a poet cry out to his God.

December 29, 2009

303

A DIFFERENT PATH

My Boy,
Your song has put me on a different path,
A path that I shall use for the good of man.

My Boy,
In pleasure and in pain,
I salute you.
I know thee as my blood.
A younger generation taking the light to the House of the Suffering Man.
When I remember the light of your song,
I love it that I cannot stop speaking of thee.
My heart is glad to its core.
What precious gift you brought.
Now that I find the prime of my life,
I shall ask nothing from thee.
Your song with such powerful rhythms shall be the strings to my heart.
Things that I have longed for came to me unexpectedly.

My Boy,
Let me be thankful to the powers that be.

December 29, 2009

A COLD NIGHT

My Boy,
This is a cold night.
I will not allow sleep to silence my thoughts.
The sharing of the words must be done.
Long life is promised to no man.

Well, then, while I breathe,
My mind is fresh.
Words, my boy, are like sweet music to my ears.
How could I not share them with you?
I have seen your spirit of boldness.
Praise God for your young mind.
Study the words that you may be able to use them.
Words, my boy, can lift the spirit.
Find the courage to stand firm.

As for me,
No cold, no heat shall dampen my spirit.
The words and only the words I pray.

December 29, 2009

THE RIGHT TIME

My Boy,
You came like fine gold to me.
You came at a time when the heart was empty.
Now that it finds its true rhythm,
I shall shape it with sweet words.

My Brothers and Sisters,
Hold on.
Even though weary,
Find the will to live.
From the dark there will be light.
Let faith be your daily food.
Lift up your hands to a higher power.

Power Higher Than I,
You have seen your children in dark waters.
Have mercy upon us.
Come forth to the rescue.
Let our eyes see the light that we may follow thee.

Blessed Father,
Forget not your children.
Let them return to praise thee.
Let sweet songs be upon their lips.
Then and there I shall weep no more.

December 30, 2009

WHO AM I TO ASK OF THEE?

When I heard the news,
Tears came to my eyes.
So young and yet she is gone
I said gone to a better place.
The Father giveth and the Father taketh.
Young or old,
The road is for all of us.
Death, the stealer of man came like a thief in the night.

Oh! Weeping Brothers and Sisters,
Let us find time to mourn the departure of our beloved.
Heaven bound, let us pray.

Blessed Father,
Everything is in your hands.
You know best.
Who am I to ask of thee?

December 31, 2009

A YEAR OF PEACE

My Boy,
You are so wonderful that your name will not leave my lips.
How can I bury my emotions?
At this hour, sleep came for me.
But I shall fight to stay awake.
Focus, my boy, shall be my cry.
I will do what is required of me.
Let me dream on to do what I am called to do.
I will not allow this mind to go to waste.
The dawn of a new year.
It's a must that I leave a new piece for your young mind.
With praying hands I look among the stars.
The great heavens I wonder.
Blessed Father,
Let this year be a year of peace and love.

January 2, 2010

I KNOW THEE

My Boy,
I know thee as my grandson.
I shall speak to thee with a grandpa's love.
Even though ripe in age,
My mind is still fresh.
The working of the mind I shall train my thoughts to find words
for your growth.
Life, my boy, is not easy.
Sometimes up, sometimes down.
The good and the bad will find thee.
Be on the alert to run away from the bad.

January 2, 2010

MY BOYS

My Boy,
I am bound by the principles of true love.
To be true to you and your brother,
How can I not love the both of you?

My Boy,
You are the eldest.
A great deal is expected of you.
Love and only true love I pray.
Be fair with your undertakings.
Your brother will be your brother.
I shall love you both.
On this night I have gone deep within my soul.
Even though cold,
I will not allow my thoughts to rest.
My love I shall put to the test.

My Boy,
Time will tell of my hands.
Let not my name escape your memory.
A song of love would be an honor.

My Boy,
I have seen so much love in you.
Share it with your brother and let Grandpa Peat be proud.

January 3, 2010

WISH NO HARM

My Boys,
Wish no harm or injuries to others.
Remember that we are all God's children.
If I cannot teach what is right,
What legacy can I leave?
What moral values would I preach?
Well, then, I shall take time out to prepare my lesson.

My Boys,
A loving heart will generate true love.
The use of the tongue should be moderate.
Boast not of your standing.
A humble man will find the courage to face his god.

Boys,
Be on the lookout for the common man.
Run away from hatred.

Boys,
With hatred taken away,
The heart will find its true rhythm.

Boys,
If I had not followed the teaching of my Father,
I would be dead to humanity.

Boys,
Go now and be Good Shepherds.

January 4, 2010

THE WORDS

My Boys,
When you look for my hands,
Look for the words.
I shall color them for your eyes.
The voice of words shall be crying out.

January 4, 2010

WHEN YOU SING

My Boy,
When you sing with the spirit,
No man shall stand in your way.
Let praises be upon the lips.
Let your goodness repair the weak hearts.
Let those with cars tune their mind on that which is good.

Oh! Great One,
Let this hour be in remembrance of thee.
In your name a young mind finds sweet words.

Oh! Loving God,
From the mouth of a child came loving words.
Rise up, my boy, and let your voice be heard.
Proud as I am,
I shall sing along.

My Boy,
My heart is happy.
Look at those eyes.
Are they not dreaming?

My Boy,
Let those that seek they face leave with peace and love.

January 4, 2010

A TRUE MAN

My Boy,
A true man will spend his life working for the common man.
Hardship or no hardship,
His mind is bent on doing good.

January 4, 2010

GIVING

My Boy,
A man who is willing to give of himself
Will find no time for idle talk.

January 4, 2010

FOR YOU AND I

My Boy,
For you and I the spreading of the words must continue.
No man in his right mind will run away from the words.
An empty soul will feed upon the words.
Man in a time of great need will use the words to cry out to his god.

January 5, 2010

THE VOICE OF A POET

When a poet finds his voice,
His singing will be sweet.
Sweeter than honey shall be his cry.
The working of the mind will be set upon the love for humanity.

My People,
Allow the poet to sing a song of love.
What sweetness finds these lips.
Let the tongue lead the way.
Come, my brothers.
Come, my sisters.
Come sing with the poet.

January 5, 2010

THE WEATHER

My Boy,
On this morning of our Lord,
The weather is brutal.
Man fighting against the fury of nature.
The cold moving on a murderous path.

My Boy,
In this plight,
Courage is a must.
As for me,
The work must be done.
The eyes of the suffering man await some good hands.
Who am I not to answer the call for duty?
Eastbound I shall go.

Blessed Father,
You have seen the task ahead.
Let me find the will to give of myself.
A loving heart will be a blessing.

Father,
Even though he falls,
Touch him that he may rise again.
Every man deserves a second chance.

Oh! Great Protector of Man,
Today I call upon thee.
The working of your hands I pray.

January 5, 2010

THE BREAK OF DAWN

At the break of dawn,
A little bird came to the window.
A song of love greeted my ears.
Why did he come?
I do not know.
I could not control my eyes.
Such sweet melodies brought me closer to its base.
Sing on, little bird.
What a glorious morning.
May your journey be safe.

January 5, 2010

DEEP MEDITATION

My Boys,
I shall pledge my time and service towards your growth.
Even though so far apart,
No distance shall dampen my love.

My Boys,
Every day I shall transmit my love.
Deep meditation will take me to where I belong.

January 5, 2010

ALL MY POEMS

My Boys,
Gather all my poems together.
Then allow one to lead.
Let it be the grand master.
Let the musicians find strings to fit the words.
Gather the children to sing a song of true love.

My Boys,
Without harmony there will be no sweetness.

My Boys,
A tune with its right notes will find the heart of man.

January 5, 2010

LOOK FOR MY HANDS

My Boys,
When you look for my hands,
Look for the words.
I shall color them for your eyes.

January 5, 2010

WHO AM I?

In the dead of night,
I rise to the sound of sweet music.

My Lord, My Lord,
Who am I not to honor thee?

January 5, 2010

BY FAITH

My Lord,
By faith I shall watch and pray.
Running stars I shall wish upon.
Let me rise up for the good of man.

January 5, 2010

WAIT FOR ME

My Dear,
I am on my way to the fountain.
What thirst finds my lips.
Cracked lips are of no use.
Wait for me.
I shall return.

January 5, 2010

WALK BY FAITH

My Boys,
Be willing to walk by faith.
Keep your eyes upon the prize.
Work to gain your wings.
If a man does not plant the seeds,
Who is he to reap the fruits?

January 5, 2010

WHO AM I NOT TO FOLLOW?

My Boy,
Your song has found a part within my soul.
I am a new man now.
I shall look at love to find its purest form.
You have opened my mind to a new concept of humanity.
What this world needs is love.
You came with love and you leave with love.
Who am I not to follow after thee?

January 6, 2010

A SONG FOR THE SOUL

Oh! Love,
Take me to the eyes of the little boy,
A boy that composes a song of love,
A song that reaches the core of the soul.
A soul that finds peace will be on the move.
Awake, my spirit.
Awake, my spirit.
Let us go on this journey.

January 6, 2010

HIDE NOT THY FACE

My Dear,
Hid not thy face from me.
You are the light,
A light that I shall use for the good of man.
Have you not eyes to see the suffering man?
Well, then, harden not your heart.
Live and let others live.

My Dear,
You know not what tomorrow will bring.
You have been blessed.
Come with me to the House of the Suffering Man.

January 6, 2010

ALL EYES

My Boy,
All eyes are upon you.
You came to this world for a purpose.
I have seen something good in you.
With your loving face,
Use it to attract the eyes.
Forget not the suffering man.
Humble yourself along life's journey.
I have seen the rise and fall of man.

My Boy,
Be prepared to be humanlike.
Live and let others live.
Find your calling,
Then work at it with a passion.
The plight of the suffering man should not escape your sight.

My Boy,
I have dedicated my life towards the suffering man.
I beg of you,
Lend me a helping hand.
My hands are getting weak now.
Rise up with your young hands and let me be proud.
Go into the world and spread the love.

January 6, 2010

TURNING MY THOUGHTS

My Boy,
As my thoughts turn to thee,
Your little face I shall follow.
For the good of man,
May you find the will to serve.
Train your young mind to feed upon that which is good.

My Boy,
A good deed will be a blessing.
Seek and find the path of the Good Shepherds.
As for me,
I cannot turn back now.
I have gone too far to turn back.
Duty and only duty shall be my cry.

My Boy,
The work must be done.
The feeding of hungry souls awaits our hands.
Let us play our part.
Let history be kind to us.

January 6, 2010

PEACE AND LOVE

My Love,
I am at the mountain.
I come to search for words that I may shape them to fit your heart.
The task ahead is not easy.
Let me turn to the sun.
Let mine eyes be on the alert.
Running words I shall put in chains.
Love and only true love shall be my cry.
Now that I am at peace,
Love will come to me.

My Love,
Here I am standing at this mountain.
Heaven-bound I allow my thoughts to go.
The sun is my witness.
Oh! Great sun, the warmer of man,
Today I shall allow my raw emotions to escape.
The gladness of this heart I shall present to the world.
Peace and love I present to the eyes that finds me.

January 6, 2010

YOU ARE THE WAY

Oh! Great Sun,
What beauty I behold this morning.
Even though the cold is murderous,
Your face shines upon man.
Oh! Great Mountain,
From this sacred spot I shall look to the east.
Blessed Father,
I come to you this morning.
Beyond the sun I shall look towards thee.
The plight of the suffering man I present to thee.
Today I took time out to cool my soul.
I cannot continue at this blistering pace.
I need to refill myself.
Father, here I am knocking at your gates.
For the good of man, speak to me.
Teach me how to write for the weary hearts.
Sweet words, my Lord, are like spice to the tongue.
Your blessing I beg of thee.
As I look at the sun,
So shall I look at thee.
Let me find words to feed the suffering man.
Father, you are the Great Master.
Lead me along the journey.
You are the way.
Open mine eyes.

January 6, 2010

BOUND BY LOVE

My Boy,
I am bound by thy love,
That I shall find words to spread the gladness of this heart.

My Boy,
On this day, before the sun rises,
I cheated the eyes from sweet sleep.
In silence I command my spirit to be still.
This mind, my boy, I put to work.
What this world needs is love.

My Boy,
You came with the light.
I shall follow thee to present the light to the eyes of man.

My People,
Where there is hatred,
Let love be its guide.

My People,
If a child can lead the way,
Why can't the elders follow?

True God,
Without love there will be no peace.
Here is my empty heart reaching to thee.
Fill me up that I may go into the world and spread the words.
Bring forth the hidden joys for the good of man.

My Lord,
At this moment I cannot move.
At your feet I beg for thy love.
The working of the mind I beg for thy guidance.
Let me find the will to share the love.

January 7, 2010

WORDS, MY BOY

My Boy,
If I write in any other tongue than that which I received,
Bad dreams would not allow me to sleep.

My Boy,
A clean heart will feed upon that which is good.
Let me give praises to the true God

My Boy,
if I cry for long life,
The work must be done.
A portion of my night is for the good of man.

My Boy,
The words from this heart shall be the light to my path.

My Boy,
When I remember the great thinkers,
Who am I not to dream on?
In silence I listen to the Great Master.
Word by word I put this hand to use.

My Lord,
There is no one to tune this man out.
Who loves me shall be with me.

January 7, 2010

FACE TO FACE

My Boy,
I shall stand before thee face to face.
A bundle of love I shall take with me.
The light of thy song of love shall be my theme song.
Play, Grandpa. Play, Grandpa.
Nice Grandpa. Nice Grandpa.

Sweet Lord,
The words from the mouth of a child.
How could I not feed upon the words?
I cry out: "My boy, give me that song again."

Blessed Father,
Let what is left of me be guided by the song of love.

January 7, 2010

A HARDENED HEART

When a man's heart gets hard,
Such a man's spirit needs to be tamed.
A search of his mind is a must.

My Friends,
Seek and find comforting words.
Feed his spirit with that which is good.
No man stands alone.
A troubled man will need some good hands.

January 7, 2010

A TROUBLED MIND

When you are confronted with a troubled mind,
It's not easy to stand firm.
A bold spirit is a must.
One needs to be careful.
In changing winds,
The proper tone of voice is a must.
One does not need to rock the boat.
It's not easy to fight against strong winds.
It's better to await its passing.
A man in a state of unrest can be dangerous.
Comforting words may lift his spirit.
Find that soft spot,
Then work on it.
If you treat a person like a human being,
Such love may find that person's heart.

My People,
Be humanlike in dealing with a troubled mind.

January 7, 2010

A LIFE WITH OTHERS IN MIND

In the sight of man and God,
My people live a life with others in mind.
No man can stand alone.
Remember we are our brother's keeper.
Do not look down on a fallen man.
We know not our end.

My People,
Be thankful of a sound mind.
I have seen madness take a hold of man,
That his pain is your pain.

My People,
All I beg of you is to do good and let good follow you.
A good deed will be a blessing.

My People,
Remember the hands of the Good Shepherds.
Follow their faith and leave this world a better place.
Let dignity be your guide.
Remember we are all God's children.
Peace and love should be our food.

My People,
With this hand I beg of you.
Remember the fallen man.

January 8, 2010

HEALING WORDS

My Boy,
I shall participate in life with my poems.
Come work with me.
Lend me your little hands.
For the good of man may I find food for the soul.

Blessed Father,
You have seen the plight of man.
The suffering I have seen is more than the eyes can bear.
Today, today I call upon thee.
Healing words I pray to find.

January 8, 2010

BY DESIGN

My Boy,
By design I bring to you a part of my heart.
Oh! Take me that I may rest well.
Promise me that my name will be upon your lips.
You and I have formed a bond.
Only God knows its true meaning.
May others learn from true love,
A love at first sight that set our minds,
A streak of light that beams from our eyes will never fade away.

January 9, 2010

FORMING MY THOUGHTS

My Boy,
At this hour sleep will not come.
I shall not allow my thoughts to run wild.
The working of the mind I shall put to use.
For the love of humanity,
May I carry the light for the children.
The old shall make a path for them to follow.

My Boy,
Safety is a must for the children.
A school of love will be a blessing to the young hearts.

Oh! Great God,
If it is thy will,
Let it be done.

My Boy,
If I find the wisdom to teach thee,
Go into the world and practice what you learn.
In the name of humanity,
Let your light shine.
I have seen something good in you.
You will be my eyes and hands for the good of man.
Yes, my boy,
At this hour I shall pray to find sweet sleep.

January 10, 2010

RACING THOUGHTS

My Boy,
I rise to find my thoughts racing to find thee.
Oh! Journey, no wind shall stop its flow.
I have set mine eyes upon the boy.
Oh! Strong love, let me find fire to my heels that I may gallop with
the wind.
The face of the boy I must see.
When a man finds happiness,
No task ahead is too great.

January 10, 2010

I WILL SEEK AFTER THEE

My Boy,
I will seek after thee for you to sing me a song of love.
If birds could do likewise,
Who am I not to stand face to face with thee.

With you my life has been blessed.
My eyes have seen a loving face.
My ears have heard your sweet voice.
I have heard the joy deep within your heart.

The good God must have sent you to bless your eyes upon your blood.
I know thee as my grandson.
What pride I do hold.
It's beyond me to refuse your tender love.
With your little hands come walk with me.
Let the code of true love bind us for the eyes to see.

My Boy,
Let us leave the rest for the historians.

January 10, 2010

LITTLE BIRDS

Two little birds came to me with wondering eyes.
Why did they come?
A song of love greeted my years.
In perfect harmony I granted my ears.
What sweet melodies ride the wind.
Sing on, little birds.
I shall not be moved.
Let the gladness of the heart find words to honor your good deed.

Oh! Wind, move not my company.
In the face of the sun I shall allow my spirit to be lifted.
The right to love I shall learn from these two little birds.

January 10, 2010

MAY PEACE BE UPON THEE

My Boy,
Word to live by...
From the stillness of the night,
Let peace be upon your lips.
Let love find a place to grow.
Find a fertile spot to plant your seeds.
Teach others how to love.
Bring out the music from within.
Let the little child sing.

January 10, 2010

A CHILD IS BORN

A child is born.
Fear not my boy.
You came to this world for a reason.
A land filled with hatred,
Yet you found time to love.
Let all men and women sing.
Play, Grandpa. Play, Grandpa.
Nice Grandpa. Nice Grandpa.
As we sing at the break of dawn,
May the angels that find thee return to the ears of God with praises.
A child is born with a loving heart.

My Boy,
The turning of my hands will be towards the heavens.
I shall cry out that you may have a long life.
You came with love and you are not afraid to give love.
What more could I ask for?
The light of the heart and mind I have seen.
May I, he holder of this pen, honor thee.

My Boy,
Now I must leave thee.
Feed upon the words.
Then go into the world and share the legacy.

January 10, 2010

I AM NOT SURE

Though I am not sure,
What do you want for your birthday?
What do you look forward to on your birthday?
I pray lots of love.
I wish you a Happy Birthday.
A song of love I shall sing for thee.
Let your friends harmonize with me.
Sail on, little Black Princess.

January 10, 2010

A DAY OF TRUE LOVE

My Dear,
I shall prepare myself.
Clean clothing I shall find.
A day of true love shall be put to the test.
Before I leave,
Let me pray.

Blessed Father,
In the spirit of true love,
Let my tongue be free.
A calm voice I beg of thee.
A song of love will be my weapon.

January 10, 2010

MY NIGHTS

My Boy,
Now my nights are yours.
As I meditate upon the words,
I pray for nothing but wisdom.
If I do not seek knowledge,
How can I teach you what is right from what is wrong?

January 10, 2010

THE HOUSE OF TRUE LOVE

My Friends,
Let us go to the House of True Love.
There awaits the eyes of a loving boy.
Let us go in peace.
Unity, my friends, I pray.

January 10, 2010

HOW I REMEMBER

My Boy,
I remember when I found that deep love.
The break of dawn I will never forget.
With great joy I shall speak thereof.
Within the confines of the elder's arms,
History was in the making.
A young mind transmitted a language of true love.
Today I salute you.
Today I honor your courage.
Your name I shall take to the eyes of man.

January 11, 2010

ONE LOVE

My Boy,
In all wisdom give God the glory.

My Boy,
If I had not awaited loved,
What heart would I carry?
When a man finds love,
All eyes will see his spirit.
His voice will be calm.
His thoughts feed upon that which is good.

My Boy,
I beg of you,
Stay away from the hands of hated.
Find your knees and ask the blessed Father for true love.
Allow your young mind to form loving words.
What this world needs is love.
If I had not fed upon my Father's teaching,
Only God knows where I would be.
How could I not honor the memory of my Father?

Boy,
They are poor.
Let them eat.
Here a man finds compassion for his brothers and sisters.

My Boy,
From this hand to yours,
Take the light and walk in love.

January 11, 2010

I AM WHO I AM

I am who I am.
Even though I am a traveling man,
The work must be done.
I shall allow my spirit its need.
The working of the mind I shall put to the test.
Let me call upon my spirit.
Awake, my spirit.
Awake, my spirit.
Let me dress myself with courage.
The eyes of the suffering man call my spirit.
Face to face I shall stand.

January 12, 2010

THE SPIRIT OF WISDOM

My Boy,
My pledge to thee...comforting words shall be my gift.
May the blessing of the Holy Father be upon thee.
Forget not to feed upon the words.
A loving heart will attract peace.

My Boy,
Learn from the words.
A wise man will know how to use his tongue.

My Boy,
Use your tongue to pray for the wisdom.
The spirit of wisdom I shall wish for thee.

January 12, 2010

I SHALL WATCH OVER THEE

My Boy,
I shall not watch over thee with closed eyes.
I have prepared myself for duty.
Well, then, my boy,
I shall stand guard.
Your growth I shall follow with keen eyes.
A song of love I shall invite others to come and sing.
Long life, my boy, I pray.
With keen eyes I shall follow your path,
A path that I pray will find the soul of humanity.

January 12, 2010

YOUR EYES

My Dear,
Your eyes are like the sun.
Your face sends a hope of love.
Use your beauty to lift the spirit of the weary souls.

My Dear,
Waste not your youth.
Come work with me.
Lend me your young hands.
Today you have seen man in a state of unrest.
Only God knows the working of his mind.
Look at his eyes dressed with wildness.
How could I not find the time to give of myself?

Blessed Father,
In your name I pray.
Remember your children.
Touch him that he may rise again.

January 16, 2010

MY INNER WORLD

My Boys,
If I do not capture my thoughts,
They will not be of any use.
My years would not be of any use to your young minds.
Let me use this mind to focus.
I shall allow my feelings to expose my inner world.
My deep love for you both,
I shall use words to magnify the working of the mind.
In silence I shall allow deep thinking its course.
Deep within my soul,
I shall allow my conscience to be true.

My God,
Be merciful to me.
As I watch and pray,
Let me follow the light.

Blessed Father,
As I follow the hands of time,
The working of the mind I shall capture before it's too late.

Little Boys,
Two heads are better than one.
For the love of humanity,
Today, today I cry out for your young hands.

Boys,
Train those hands for the good of man.
Today I am leaving a part of me that you both may look at the
working of the mind.

January 16, 2010

WHAT SHALL I DO?

My Boy,
At this hour I await the sun.
No tears shall dampen my eyes.
The work must be done.
The weary souls must be fed.

Oh! Great Father,
As I look to thee,
You have seen the desire of this heart.
For the good of man,
Lead me to the fountain of love.
I have seen hatred jumping like frogs,
The tongue in use like a sharp sword,
His lips moving hatred with a passion.

Father,
What shall I do?

Oh! Great Father,
Teach me thy ways.
Now that my mind is fresh,
Give unto me the desire of my heart.
Let me run with the words for the good of man.
Man in his plight of desperation has gone mad.

My Lord,
On this beautiful morning,
I present my hands to thee.
Teach me thy ways.

January 16, 2010

A LOOK AT MY LIFE

My Boys,
Today I shall look at my own life for a change.
From my youth I have used these hands for the good of man.
From where did I get this idea?
When I remember my Father's teaching,
How grateful I am.
A young mind captured that which is good.
The House of Higher Learning I could not resist.

My Boys,
Goals upon goals I moved along.
The love for humanity became my pet.

My Boys,
A loving heart will lead to success.
The spirit of my Father will never leave.
How could I turn away from His guidance?
What conscience would I put on display?
What legacy would I leave for thee?
What footsteps would I leave for you to follow?

My Boys,
If you should find my hands,
Today at sunrise I leave my marks.

My Boys,
Let nothing get between your hearts.
The work must be done.
Keep your ancestors' spirits alive.

January 16, 2010

WHY SHOULD I START?

My Dear,
If I cannot give my heart,
Why should I start?
Why should I look to take my mind,
When a mind is free from added burdens?
The beating of the heart will be light.
Only a fool will boast of a heavy heart.
At this hour, from my quiet space,
A taste of fellowship is more than I.
Awake from dreams that took this body beyond my control.
I shall now regroup.
I will not allow bitterness a place to grow.

My Dear,
If I dream of great things,
The work must be done.
My goals are mine to keep.
Well, then, if I do not allow these eyes rest,
Forgive me.
The work must be done.

My Dear,
In silence I put this mind to work.
Dreams or no dreams,
I shall go forth.

January 17, 2010

PLOT YOUR COURSE

If a man cannot plot his own course,
Then others will do likewise.
Have I not a mind of my own?
Am I not my own captain?
The waters I choose I shall set sail upon.
Every man should find his calling.
Find the burning desire to go on your mission.
Life is short.
Run with the wind.
Call upon the true God for guidance.

January 17, 2010

A JOYFUL HEART

My Boy,
When I saw the joy of your heart,
What sweet music came from thee.
My Boy,
In pleasure I stand.
You have brought me the light.
I came to thee in darkness,
And now I have seen the light.
My Boy,
I shall carry this light to the eyes of man.
All evil spells shall be driven from this heart.
Blessed Father,
A new heart of true love I pray.
I shall cover my feet with the peace sign.
My Boy,
At the center of this heart,
Your loving face strikes.
The good God must have sent you at this crucial moment.
My Boy,
I shall leave a new man.
My Boy,
In prayers I shall call upon your name,
A name that dances upon my tongue.
When I remember how I stood before thee face to face,
Your loving smile set me on fire.
My Boy,
Welcome your dignity.
Even though you speak not,
This heart received a bundle of joy.
My Boy,
I shall go now.
The world awaits the tales with your song of love.
Play, Grandpa. Play, Grandpa.
Nice Grandpa. Nice Grandpa.

January 17, 2010

TAKING THE WORDS

My Boys,
I shall take time out from my quiet moment.
My love for you both must be told.
Now that I have found my new love,
I have found a new spirit.

My Boys,
I will now dress myself in clothing of true love.
My tongue will not rest.
The words I shall take to the heart of my friends.
A song of love I shall compose.
I will allow my heart to beat with pride.

My Boys,
The little that is left of me,
Kind words will be my cry.
Now that I have tasted true love,
May the God I serve allow me to taste wisdom.
The minds of these young boys I pray to feed upon.

My Boys,
If the birds could sing for me,
Who am I not to ask the both of you to sing for me too?

My Boys,
A song of love would be a blessing to this old soul.
Play, Grandpa. Play, Grandpa.
Nice Grandpa. Nice Grandpa.
Those words I shall take with me.

January 18, 2010

THE EARTH

My God,
When the earth burst,
Man was no match for its belly.
Faces that were once filled with hatred,
Now drip tears like raindrops.

My God, My God,
How long can the hands of hatred last?
Yes, man confronted the hands of the Great Ruler.
The hoarding of fine gold lines the frames of the dead.
Fire moves everything in its path.
A nation is under the spell of disaster.
Now its people are crying out to God.
I have seen man raising his fist toward the heavens,
Begging the true God for mercy.

Blessed Father,
Mine eyes have become heavy.
The burden of man is making a mockery of my old heart.

Blessed Father,
Awake the spirit of the living.

January 18, 2010

THE WORDS

Awake, my spirit.
Awake, my spirit.
To the East I must await the face of the sun.

Oh! Great Father,
The voice of the suffering man will not leave.

My Lord, My Lord,
What shall I do?
The working of the mind I do not understand.
What madness I have seen.

Father,
What shall I do?
Here I come to thee a broken man.
Let me pray for thy hands.
Teach me that I may learn they ways.

Father,
At this hour, here are my hands.
As I look beyond the face of the sun,
From your great heavens speak to me.
The eyes of the suffering man await my hands.

Holy Father,
Spur me that I may run with the words.
Healing words I beg of thee.

Father,
The sun has its work to do.
As for me,
The work must be done.
Who am I to refuse my calling?
To the House of the Suffering Man I must go.
Let me carry the words to cool the weary soul.

January 18, 2010

I CANNOT BE SILENT

My Boys,
I cannot be silent when the work must be done.
Mine eyes are full with the pain of the suffering man.
How long, my Lord, how long, my Lord,
Can I hold the strain?

My Boys,
My hands are getting weak now.
I shall ask the both of you, in the name of humanity,
Lend me your young hands.

My Boys,
Love and peace are the key.
At this hour I am at the mountain.

Boys,
Let us dedicate our service towards humanity.
Let me pray, blessed Father.
Let these two boys make the right choice.
As for me, I cannot turn back now.
Today, my Lord, my faith I put into your hands.
As I look towards thee,
The sun is my witness.
The soul of humanity I present to thee.

January 18, 2010

GIVE ME A CHANCE

Give me a chance to open my mind.
Only God knows its inner workings.
I shall use this mind for the good of man.

My People,
I shall look for words to feed the soul.
Man by himself will attract madness.
I have seen madness in full bloom.
If you are not strong,
It will take you along.
A broken mind will need fixing.

Blessed Father,
I do not know how to fix the mind.
Let me find comforting words to heal its pain.
Now that I have exposed my emotions,
Father, let me not be ashamed.
I come to you a humble man.
Just concern about my brothers and sisters.
I cannot turn my eyes away from the suffering.
The pain I pray to endure.

My People,
I will allow my conscience to take me along.

January 18, 2010

THE SCORN OF HUMAN SUFFERING

My Boys,
The scorn of human suffering leaves a nation in limbo.
Where are the Good Shepherds?
When will man learn to be his brother's keeper?

Power Higher Than I,
In light of the great sorrows,
Have mercy upon a fallen nation.
Let its people find the will to rise again.

Father,
You have seen the state of confusion,
The blood of its people staining the land.

My God,
When will it end?
When will man return to praise thee?
I have seen the dead in numbers.
Weeping and moaning all over the land,
A land of death,
A land of great suffering.

Blessed Father,
Hold back your hands that man may come back to thee.

January 18, 2010

I ENTER MY HEART

When I enter my heart for these two boys,
I am drinking from the fountain of love.
I find pleasure searching for words to fit their hearts.

My God,
How long I have waited for love.
Today pride took a hold of me.

January 18, 2010

PARTING WORDS ONE LOVE

My People,
The voice of a poet is speaking.
A vision of peace and love I pray.
In the spirit of human dignity,
I shall use these fingers to speak thereof.
My journey has been long from my land to this land.
We are all God's children.
The song of my heart I shall bring to the weary souls.
How could I not envision a land of peace and prosperity?

My People,
If I lend these hands to fight a just cause,
Come fight with me.

My Brothers and Sisters,
The task ahead will not be easy.
Let us pray to find the hands of God.

Oh! Heavenly Father,
You have seen the plight of your people.
How troubled I am.

Father,
Through you all things are possible.
Today, today I call upon you.
Hear our cries.
Have mercy upon your people.

Father,
let they light shine that they may follow.
Let unity be upon their lips.

My People,
My parting words shall be "one love."

January 19, 2010

A PLACE TO COOL OFF

My Friends,
I have seen the greed of man.
Man storing his earthly gains,
Then using his lips to boast of his status.
A fool will always be a fool.
I have seen the fall of man,
That madness took a hold of him.
Who is man that I should be afraid?
Here today and tomorrow he is gone.

My Friends,
Take heed.
I have seen birds take over the belongings of man,
Singing a song of freedom.

My Friends,
Watch your steps.
Find the will to give.
Find the will to love.
Live a life that others may follow.
Today I look at man behaving as if he owns this land.
Poor fool not knowing that the land awaits what is left of him.

Yes, My Friends,
I shall go to the mountain.
Dancing trees and singing birds will cool my wrath.

January 19, 2010

GRANDPA, GRANDSONS' POEM

My Boys,
It's me.
Not your Father.
Not your Mother.
It's me, Grandpa Peat.

My Boys,
Allow me to speak to your young minds.
I shall speak from a loving heart.
As I follow the hands of time,
Your faces will not leave my memory.
With this hand I shall leave my love.

Boys,
Stand by me to do that which is good.

Boys,
Bring me your love.
A loving heart is all I need.
My soul will find its richness,
Then I shall find a song of love.
Come with your little voices that we may sing along.

January 19, 2010

STANDING FIRM

I will not allow any man to hold me down.
The work must be done.
At the break of dawn,
I will find the will to press on.
For the good of man I rise.

Power Higher Than I,
Here I am.
Let me follow the light to the House of Suffering.
Faces that once caused heads to turn,
Now refuse to bring out the beauty from within.

Blessed Father,
Today I call upon thee.
You have seen your children in great need.
Be merciful to them.
Lift their spirits that they may smile again.
As for me,
Let me pray for courage to give of myself.
Day by day I shall press on.

January 19, 2010

A HOPE OF LOVE

My Dear,
Your eyes are like the sun.
Your face sends a hope of love.
Use your beauty to lift the spirit of the weary souls.

My Dear,
Waste not your youth.
Come work with me.
Lend me your young hands.
Today you have seen man in a state of unrest.
Only God knows the working of his mind.
Look at his eyes dressed with wildness.
How could I not find the time to give of myself?

Blessed Father,
In your name I pray.
Remember your children.
Forget not this man.
Touch him that he may rise again.

January 19, 2010

THE JOY WITHIN

My Boys,
The joy within I shall let it be known.
Grandpa's love shall be coated in words.
I always pray for a good ending.
How proud I am to be thankful.
With boastful lips I shall sing a song of true love.

My God,
What else could I ask for?
They are my blood.
The ancestors' spirits live on.

January 19, 2010

WHAT AM I LIVING FOR?

If I cannot give of myself,
What am I living for?
What footsteps would I leave for my boys to follow?
With this hand,
I pledge my years for the good of man.

My Boys,
The road I choose is not an easy road.
Along my journey,
The eyes of the suffering man will never leave this heart.
The words of my Father are like music to the ears.
"Boy, do what you can to help the poor."
How could I forget this man?

January 20, 2010

THE WORK OF YOUR HANDS

My Boys,
You are the children of my blood.
Therefore you are my blood.
I pray that true love will be upon your hearts.
As for me,
I shall pray for the blessing of your hands.

My Boys,
Let your lights shine for the soul of humanity.

Boys,
Shut not your eyes upon the suffering man.
Find the will to love.
Find the will to give of yourselves.
Allow the spirits to find your hands.

January 20, 2010

A JUST PATH

My Boys,
Follow the path of that which is just.
Step away from the hands of evil.
Seek and find the fountain of love.
Turn not away from the weary souls.

My Boys,
At this hour I am under the stars.
I shall call upon the Lord for comforting words.

My Boys,
What this world needs is love.
If I cannot teach the heart of true love,
Why should I live?
The words of the Most High must be upon your lips.
This world will be a better place with some good hands.

Boys,
Seek and find the hands of the Good Shepherds.
Walk within the laws of the Most High.
Run away from the streets of hatred.

My Boys,
Be at peace with your God.
Set your eyes upon the prize,
Then work towards gaining your wings.

January 21, 2010

MY BELOVED

Come, my dear,
Come to the Fountain of Love.
Come drink with me.
Fear not, my dear.
The power of love will never leave.
Let me sing a song of love for thy ears.

Oh! Sweet Little Honeybee,
Take me to your place that I may wet my tongue.
Let your sweetness fatten my heart.

January 21, 2010

OUR STEPS

My Boys,
When the time is right,
Go to the Book of Love.
Feed upon the words,
Then invite others to come forth.

My Boys,
Comforting words are like food to the soul.
I cannot stop now.
I have seen the suffering in the eyes of man.
My spirit cannot rest.

My Boys,
Come work with me.
Your young minds will be a blessing.

Boys,
I have seen the love in your faces.
Let's go to the heart of the suffering man.
Let's set our eyes upon the prize.
Gaining our wings is a must.
For the love of humanity,
Let us find the courage to give of ourselves.
Let us unite to fight for a just cause.
Our steps, I pray, will line with dignity.

January 27, 2010

STRIKE ME

My Love,
Play for me.
Strike me with those keys.
Let each key speak to me.
Fine-tune your rhythm that I may be whole again.
Let the power of your hands cool my spirit.

January 27, 2010

GREAT DREAMS

My Boys,
I am a traveling man.
At night sweet sleep is of the past.

Blessed Father,
Let me live to follow the growth of the boys.
Great dreams I wish to dwell upon.

January 27, 2010

LET ME FIND MY STAR

Father,
As I sit on this holy ground,
Remember this traveling man,
A man from a far away land,
A man searching the heavens for thee.
When I remember the burden of man,
Mine eyes are full.
My heart I cannot control.
Now that I lift up mine eyes to thee,
Take me to the well that I may refresh my spirit.
Hit me with the spirit of love that I may dance to please the
suffering man.

Father,
Now that I lift up my love to thee,
Give unto me the fire I need.

True God,
Help me to serve.

Father,
As I cry out to thee,
Let me find my star.

January 27, 2010

THE SPIRIT OF TRUE LOVE

My Boy,
I have seen your true spirit,
A loving face that attracts the eyes.

Heavenly Father,
In the name of human dignity,
May the pursuit of his young mind work upon that which is good.

My Lord,
If I should teach,
May I find the right words to lift the spirits.

My Boy,
I have seen man in a state of unrest.
Seek to improve social justice.
Waste not your years upon vanity.
When the time is right,
Only the earth will gain.

Well, then, my boy, as I speak,
You have shown the heart of true love.
May others find the time to learn.
As for me, I shall find words to honor thee.

My Boy,
The spread of true love is a must.
What this world needs is peace and love.
If a child can lead the way,
So be it.

January 29, 2010

LET ME PRAY

My Boy,
For the suffering man I shall speak up.
I will not fold my hands in the face of human dignity.
I will allow conscience to take its course.
If I cannot stand for justice,
Why should I live?
What honor would I leave upon my father's name?

My Boy,
If you feed a child upon that which is good,
Such a child will produce that which is good.

My Boy,
If I teach thee well,
Find the courage to spread the legacy.
Remember to go to the heart of the children.

My Boy,
Do not be afraid.
Remember a child shall lead the way.

My Boy,
What this world needs are some good hands.

My Boy,
Go now and prepare yourself.
Let me pray.

Blessed Father,
At this hour I stand alone.
Your work must be done.
Let this boy find the courage to serve.
Then and there I shall weep no more.

January 29, 2010

OLD HANDS

My Boy,
I have seen old hands that hurt no more.
A man can only do so much.
Time, my boy, is the master.

My Boy,
I have seen strong winds that fade away.
Who is man that I should be afraid?

My Boy,
In my book a spade will be a spade.

Blessed Father,
Along life's journey,
I pray for clean hands.
Loving hands, my Lord, will be a blessing.
The soul of humanity is in great need.

January 29, 2010

IS DEATH THE ANSWER?

My People,
I shall try to keep it clean but fair.
The level of hatred running across the land.

My Lord,
How long shall man run wild?
How can he be tamed?
Is death the only answer?

January 29, 2010

A SOUL ON FIRE

My Love,
Before I come to thee,
Let me find the sun to warm my spirit.
When I set my soul on fire,
My feet will find its rhythm.
If a song of love takes a hold of me,
Do not be afraid.
I have atoned myself.
The eyes of man will see a new man.

Oh! Mountain,
You have heard a lover's cry.
May the winds be witness.

January 29, 2010

YOUNG BLOOD

My Boy,
You have shown what can be done in the face of hatred.
A loving heart will find the fire it needs.
A mind that is under the guidance of the Most High will be a blessing
to humanity.

My Boy,
I have seen hatred breed war upon war.
Man refused to find the will to love.

My Boy,
When greed takes a hold of man,
He will trade his soul for fine gold.
A fool will be a fool.
I have seen the fall of man,
That the birds took a hold of him.

My Boy,
When will man learn to live a life that others may follow?

My Boy,
Peace and justice I pray.
You have seen the light.
Walk with the light that others may follow.

True God,
You have seen this young mind.
Let him live to do your work.
I have seen the fire on his spirit.
Young blood is what the world needs.

January 29, 2010

I PRAY FOR PEACE AND LOVE

My Child,
Allow me to speak.
I have seen the eyes of man going wild,
The once mighty fall from grace.
Today I look at man in another house.
What pity I have seen.
A tongue that once spit fire now ceases to perform.
Oh! What a shame.
The mighty become lame.

My Child,
Boast not of your high standing.
Be soft on your tongue.
Let your work speak for you.
You came with nothing and you shall leave with nothing.

My Child,
I beg of thee,
Find the will to love.
Love, my child, will create peace.
You have seen nation against nation,
War upon war destroying the land.
Its people carrying the baggage of sorrows.

My God,
When will it end?
When will your children find the will to live in harmony?
Today I pray for peace and love.

January 30, 2010

I AM AFRAID

My Dear,
How I am afraid of those false tongues.
Self-hatred pulls my lips.
Man chooses evil over good.

January 30, 2010

THE JOURNEY

My Boy,
No matter the journey,
No man will stop his mind from preaching to thee.
A house of words I shall leave for your young eyes.
Seek and find the House of Wisdom.

January 30, 2010

THE EAST

Oh! Great East,
As I come to thee,
Sweet music I bring.
My heart I set upon finding words to uplift man.
Along, my God, I look to thee.
Here are my hands.
Write with me.
Yes, the burden of man holds me down.
As I await the rising sun,
The moon I shall follow.

Father,
From your high place,
Forget not this man.
Let me live to find the food I need.

Oh! Darkness,
The light I shall await.
Sweet music will be my lover.
Let this heart follow its rhythm.

My Friends,
At the rock I stand.
Let the gladness of this heart feed upon the words.

January 30, 2010

YOU CAN MOVE ANY EYES

My Dear,
With those lips,
You can move any eyes.
Work them for the love of humanity.
Use your gift to bring joy to the weary souls.
Be thankful of what you received.
Come, my dear,
Come work with me.
I shall keep watch over thee.
I will not allow evil hands near thee.

My Dear,
Let us do the job.
The work must be done.

January 30, 2010

THE LIGHT OF THE SUN

My Boy,
The sun and its light I cannot leave.
The dark I cannot stand.
Oh! What a beautiful morning.
Man and birds finding a common ground.
Tress that were once still now dancing to the tune of the winds.

Oh! Great One,
Here I am.
At the rock I present my hands.
Help me to carry the light,
A light that may brighten the eyes of the suffering man.

My God,
I am just a traveling man with a big heart.
The voice of truth I cannot allow to be silent.
From my bed here I am crying out to thee.
If only I could find the right words.
My night would be sweet.

January 30, 2010

AWAKE, MY LOVE

Awake, my love.
The hands of the children await thy hands.
You must go now before it's too late.

January 31, 2010

WASTE NO TEARS

My Boy,
When I am dead,
Tell them to waste no tears for me.
Tears, my boy, will be of no use.
A man needs tears when he can see the raw emotions.

My Boy,
My life was built within the confines of the suffering man.
Their pain and pleasure I have seen with these two eyes.

My Boy,
Without deep love,
The heart cannot carry the weight.
Now I am in a state of maturity.
My years I shall use to guide me along.

My Boy,
At the end of the journey,
If you do not leave good deeds,
Your name might not find the tongue of others.
Well, then, I have prepared my hands.
When the time is right,
Remember the words feed upon them.
Forget not the heart of the children.
Feed them upon that which is good.

February 1, 2010

IN THE NAME OF POETRY

My Boy,
In the name of poetry I shall allow my thoughts to follow
the great poets.
The search for truth I shall pray upon.
Even though I do not understand the behavior of man,
The work must be done.

Oh! Great Ruler of Man,
From my knees I rise to ask of thee,
Let me feed upon the words.
A vision of great ideas I dream of.

February 1, 2010

THIS LOVE

My Boy,
This love of mine I shall put in cast for thee.
Years to come,
You shall see the light.

February 2, 2010

WHY WORRY?

When you cannot sleep,
Fix your heart upon something sweet.
Empty your heart of the dead weight.
A heart filled with heavy burdens will corrupt the mind.

My People,
The things that you cannot control,
Why waste your time to worry?
Find something good to feed the spirit.
As for me,
I shall feed upon the words.
I came with nothing,
And I shall leave with nothing.

February 2, 2010

SWEET TONGUE

My Dear,
With your sweet tongue I shall follow thee like a bee.
I will not allow strong winds to beat me down.
Victory and only victory shall be my cry.

February 2, 2010

372

THIS WORLD

My Boy,
This world is not an easy place to live,
But life goes on.
Learn to deal with the bitter and the sweet.

My Boy,
Humility is a must.
Along life's journey there will be pain and pleasure.
Moderation is the key to success.

My Boy,
At all times keep your eyes upon the prize.
Set your compass, then move along.
Leave hatred alone.
Do not burden yourself with such baggage.
Use your mind to cultivate that which is good.
Only a fool boasts of his standing.

My Boy,
Life is short.
Leave something good.
Open your heart to those in need.

My Boy,
Plant your seeds that you may reap your fruits.
A man living a life without good deeds,
Only the earth will claim him.

February 2, 2010

A MIND ON FIRE

My Boy,
Today I am at my best.
The working of the mind is on fire.
Even though lame,
The work must be done.
The words, my boy, I cannot keep.
Why should I hide my music when I am a free man to sing along?

My Boy,
Sweet music is good for the spirit.
A man finding his passion will not waste his time.

My Boy,
Time awaits no man.

February 2, 2010

GO AND STUDY THE WORDS

My Boy,
When I am gone,
I beg of you to go and study the words.

My Boy,
Feed upon the words,
Then take them to the heart of man.
Today I am reaching for the core of my soul.
My spirit cannot rest until I put the words in chains.
In this cold, my boy,
The work must be done.
You will be my eyes and ears.

My Boy,
If you find tears upon the words,
Do not be ashamed.
Go and teach the children.

My Boy,
I have seen the love you generate.
Use that love for the good of man.
If I cannot use this hand to direct your path,
Why should I be thankful for my years.
Well, then, my boy,
One good morning my work will speak for me.

February 2, 2010

WONDERS

My Boy,
I cannot believe the moon competing with the sun.
Morning stars made a mockery of what I have seen.
The great heavens and its wonders I ponder.

Oh, Great God,
Your work is in full view.
As I meditate upon this boy,
I ask of thee,
Let him follow the path of the Good Shepherds.
True love I pray he will carry along.
For the good of man may he see the light.
With his young mind may he find the will to lead.
Bless his heart that he may find the courage.
Let him walk with dignity.
As I follow the formation of the clouds,
My thoughts I form around this boy.
I will not allow my spirit to get cold.
Awake, my spirit.
Awake, my spirit.
The voice of the boy is calling.
There is no time to sit idle.
The work must be done.

February 2, 2010

GREAT THINKING

My Boy,
Dream like I have no other choice.
Great thinking took a hold of me.
I will not rest until I reach the Promised Land,
A land of great thinkers.

My Boy,
The road will not be easy.
I shall clothe myself with great faith,
Then allow my spirit to find that passion.

My God,
I pray that I may enter the House of Wisdom.
When I remember the children,
Where are the good teachers?
A young mind needs good food for its growth.

My Boy,
I took great pride in my thinking.
The purity of the mind I set towards the soul of humanity.

Oh! Great God,
Help me to use this mind for the good of man.

February 2, 2010

BOASTED AMONG FRIENDS

My Boy,
If I could only play upon the harp,
What sweetness I would bring to your ears.
A song of love would be my choice.

My Boy,
You came to me singing.
Play, Grandpa. Play, Grandpa.
Nice Grandpa. Nice Grandpa.
Those words, my boy, became music to my ears.
The gladness of the heart I could not control.
Now I am a new man.
I boasted among friends of thy true love.
I find pleasure in thinking that God must have sent you.
Even though too young to understand,
No one could stop the power of love.

My Boy,
I rise before the sun.
From my quiet place,
Your face will never leave.
How could I not capture this moment?

Blessed Father,
You have seen the love in this boy.
May the angels take him along his journey.

My Boy,
Now that the sun is upon me,
Let me follow the light.
I shall sing a song of love to honor thee.

February 3, 2010

LET ME BE GOOD

As I look towards the heavens,
Father, may I find your ears.
Today I shall speak to thee from the heart.
What I have seen in the House of Suffering turns my stomach.
Let me be a good man.
Let me find the will to love.

February 3, 2010

GO TO THE HOUSE OF GOD

My Boy,
Go to the House of God.
A mother's words that will never leave.

Oh! Mother,
May your spirit be always with me.
Today I set my heart upon your tender hands.
What comfort they were to me.
With this hand I shall honor thee.
Sweet words I shall frame for thee.
My years have been blessed.

My Dear Mother,
For the love of humanity I salute you.
Your teaching I shall take to the world.
Now that I am in a far away land,
Your words are with me.
Your love for the children I shall continue.

Mother,
The long journey I took is because of your loving hands.
From now on there shall be no turning back.
Your wish shall be granted.
Now I am more than ready for my journey.

February 3, 2010

LOOKING AT MAN

When I looked at man in another house,
A part of me wept.
The fall of man was in full view.
A mind that once fed upon great things,
Now ceases to find good reasoning.

My God,
You have seen what I have seen.
What shall I do?
Let me find the courage to stand firm.
Let me find the heart to serve.
In the name of human dignity,
Let me find the heart to love.

Blessed Father,
In this house,
Without love there is no hope.
Let me find the courage to lend a helping hand.

Oh! Great Protector of Man,
Here I am.
Let me find the fire I need.
The return of man I pray.
Today I come before thee a humble man.
You have seen the desire of this heart.
If only I could find the right words,
A song of love would be upon my lips.

Oh! Great One,
Come to our rescue.

February 24, 2010

THE GRATITUDE OF THIS HEART

My Boys,
With the gratitude of this heart,
Let me pray.

Oh! Heavenly Father,
In Your name I present these two boys.
For the love of humanity,
May their young minds feed upon that which is good.
For the good of man,
Help them to find the will to serve.
May their years be long.
As for me,
Sweet words I shall take to them.

My Boys,
Even though young at heart,
Seek and find the House of the Good Shepherds.

My Boys,
Draw from their wisdom.
Today I am in the House of the Suffering Man.
What pain I have seen.

My Boys,
The work must be done.
Hide not your hands from the suffering man.
Let dignity be your guide.
Rise up and do that which is good in the name of humanity.

My Boys,
Go into the world and spread the love.
Let me be proud.

February 24, 2010

A MIND IN SHAPE

My Boys,
To keep my mind in shape,
I feed upon the words that my tongue will be in shape.
A loose tongue only brings disgrace.

March 3, 2010

THE LIGHT

My Boys,
On this night,
The rhythm of this heart I set for your ears.
The working of the mind I shall train to produce that which is good.

True God,
At this hour,
Running stars I shall cast my wishes.

Great Moon,
Your face I have seen.

Heavenly Father,
For the good of man I pray.
I come to thee this night.
The name of these two boys I present to thee.
For the love of humanity,
Bless their hearts that they may find the will to love.
Without a loving heart,
The work cannot be done.

My Boys,
Duty and only duty will be my cry.
My hands I have prepared for thee.
My heart I have trained to beat towards thee.

Boys,
If I cannot carry the light,
How could I ask for thee to follow?

March 9, 2010

NO PAIN

My Boys,
Without any pain,
I shall allow this hand to speak for me.
On the plight of man,
I have seen man allow hatred to turn him into a monster.
His lips move like pistons towards his evil deeds.
Man in his mad state causes a whole nation to call upon God.

My God,
You have seen man falling apart.
What shall I do?
How long, my God...
How long shall the wicked hands continue?
In this state of panic,
Where are the Good Shepherds?
Where are the changes for good?
When will man allow good reasoning to be his tool?

Spirit of the Most High,
Today I call upon thee.
Come to the aid of man.
I have seen man go stiff stone mad,
Turning himself into a pillow of fire.

March 10, 2010

REAPERS OF WORDS

In my quiet time,
I put this mind to work.
Finding words is all I pray.
Attention reapers of words,
Let me be proud by putting them on display.
True love will be my theme.
If your heart is not right,
Get in tune with a song of love.
When a man finds love,
A happy heart will be his reward.

My People,
Be true to yourself.
Let no man dampen your spirit.
A mean dressed in love will attract the eyes of others.
What more could a man ask for but to be loved?

My People,
A loving heart will generate peace.

My People,
Without love there can be no peace.
Come elders,
Set the stage for the children to play.
Let your names become a theme song.
A song of love will be a blessing.

March 10, 2010

MY DEAR, FOLLOW ME

My Dear,
Follow me.
Come, let us go to the House of Pain.
There awaits the eyes of the fallen.

My Dear Father,
You have seen the task ahead.
Help me not to be afraid.
Pulling eyes I cannot escape.

Blessed Father,
Help me to stand firm.
I cannot turn back now.
I have come from a far away land knowing that the work must be done.
If I could only find some good hands,
My day would be sweet.
Westbound I shall go.

Oh! Great Sun,
Your light I shall follow.
A warm spirit I shall ask of thee.
When I remember the task ahead,
The swelling of my head I cannot control.

Power Higher Than I,
Here I am.
Take me to where I belong.

March 10, 2010

LAND OF MY BIRTH

My Boys,
How could I not be who I am?
Today I stand alone before the sun.
I shall allow my thoughts to find thee.

My Boys,
The land of my birth,
There you are.
May the spirits of the ancestors touch your young minds.

My Boys,
Heap no shame upon your roots.
Go and study their path.
Get a feel for their spirit.
As for me,
I shall teach their rich history.

Land of My Birth,
Your son cries out from a far away land.
Even though I turned my back upon your soil,
I shall not be ungrateful to my people.
Young souls I have sent with my love.
Today I make plans to come to my roots.

Oh! Great Father,
You have seen this man.
Today I have gone within myself.
Tomorrow the iron bird will take me to the land of my birth.
There awaits the eyes of the young souls.

March 17, 2010

MY BOYS, I SPEAK TODAY

My Boys,
I speak today to the souls of men.
I have seen man and how far he is gone.
Poor souls laden with pain.

My God,
When will he come back to thee?
Where is thy message?
I pray soon, little boys,
Harden not your hearts.
I shall take this moment to speak to your young souls.
I will make myself a humble man.
At the mountain I stand.
East bound I allow my thoughts to go beyond the sun.
The ears of God I pray to reach.

My Boys,
All my trust I shall rest upon your young minds.
I will give my years of knowledge.

My Boys,
Please be consistent with true love.
A troubled man may not have the ability to think for himself.

My Boys,
Obedience will be necessary to do the Father's work.

My Boys,
The task ahead will not be easy.
However, the work must be done.

My Boys,
I do not expect perfection.

My Boys,
Go into the world and think for yourselves.
Let me be proud of my hands.

March 17, 2010

THE QUEEN

My Dear,
You are the beauty of this place.
You are the Queen and all honors belong to you.
What joy you brought to the suffering eyes.
The good God must have sent you.
Your presence lifted our spirits.
Long live our dear Queen.

My people, let us sing a song for our dear Queen.
We came with nothing, but we found your true love.
Oh! Love, lift up our spirits.
Our Queen is in the house.
Look, my dear people, birds and all came to grace the ears of
our dear Queen.
Long live the Queen.

My God, we cannot beg for more.
You gave us our Queen.
What more can we ask for?
My people, come, let us sing a song of love.
Blessed Father, you gave us the whole world.
The Queen, my Lord, we present to thee.

My People, who are you praying for?
The Queen, the Queen.
Father, long life we beg of thee.

March 19, 2010

389

TODAY I CRY TO THEE

My Lord, My Lord,
Today I cry to thee.
Oh! Land of my birth,
Your son came back to his roots.
How could I not remember my roots?
From the fat of the land,
Here I am a grown man.
For the good of man,
My Father's teaching I shall put into practice.

Boy, remember the poor.
Harden not your hands.
Remember to be humanlike.
If you see a man and he is hungry, my boy,
Then turn not your head.
You have seen my hands.
On your journey,
Speak no evil thereof.

My boy, follow your dreams.
Go into the world and do what is expected of you.
Let your lips be moved with praises.
Yes, my people, the voice of my Father will never leave.
Now that I await the iron bird,
What sweet memories I hold for the good of man.

Blessed Father, for the love of humanity,
Teach me thy ways.
Today I set my compass.
May your angels keep watch.

March 24, 2010

LEND ME YOUR HANDS

My Boys,
Lend me your hands.
For the good of man,
Come work with me.
In my state of old glory,
The work must be done.

Boys,
Let me be proud.
This world is full of hatred.
Let peace and love be your choice.
Today I am at the core of my soul,
In sight of the Most High.
I beg for your hands.
Come, let us go and do the Father's work.
Use your minds to uplift the spirit of the fallen man.
True love, my boys, will be your weapon.
If I cannot speak the truth,
What legacy will I leave?
Well, then,
This is my hand.
May you both be pleased.
I shall go snow.
Remember the work must be done.

April 11, 2010

A POET'S CRY

The Sun and I,
Oh! Beauty, from your heavenly stay,
I have witnessed your light.
Today I stand before your face.
How grateful I am to rise this morning.
For the good of man,
Let me pray.

Blessed Father,
At this hour I come before thee a humble man.
The burden of man I cannot understand.
I have seen the head of man begging for mercy.
A mind that once reasoned with purity,
Is now in the hands of others.
What pity I have seen.

Oh! Great Healer,
Come forth.
May your hands be upon his head.
Your mercy, my Lord, I pray.
Take away this burden that he may return to his rightful mind.
Let his lips find praises for thee.

As for me,
I can only lend a helping hand.
In secret I come to thee this morning.
The sun is my witness.

April 12, 2010

A MOTHER'S LOVE

From the wondering eyes,
The true meaning of love penetrated her aging face.
He is mine.
How could I not love him?
What is mine is mine.

My Friends,
Even though I cannot escape the pain,
I shall await what pleasure I find.
Only God knows the burden I bear.
I shall remain faithful to my blood.
Who am I not to do what is expected of me?

Blessed Father,
In full view I present my case.
Great healing I beg of thee.
Even though my heart is full,
Spare me that I may give of myself.
A mother's love cannot cease.
I will not allow pride to blind my eyes.
Good or bad,
I am who I am.
Grant unto me the courage to stand in the face of danger.
I cannot allow my blood to go to waste.

April 17, 2010

FORGET NOT YOUR DESCENDANTS

My Boys,
Forget not your descendants.
Go to your roots and study their paths.

Oh! Young Bloods,
Allow not pride to take you along the wrong road.
Go to the House of the Elders.

My Boys,
Listen and learn from their years of experience.
An old head is full of knowledge.
Old eyes will not forget the dark.

My Boys,
Without the light,
One cannot see.
Life will never be the same.

Father of all Lights,
Today I look to thee.
The working of the mind I set upon the sun.
Clearance I beg of thee.
May the sweetness of my spirit move me to teach the young souls.

Sun, the Ruler of All Lights,
Now that I have seen your beauty,
I shall not be afraid of the dark.
I will not hold my tongue to speak about the light.

Boys,
Go now and find oil for the burning lamp.

April 18, 2010

HOLD YOUR HEADS HIGH

My Boys,
Soon you will be asked to go out into the world.
Do not be afraid.
Hold your heads high.
Find that courage to comfort the heart.

Boys,
Treat others with dignity.
A song of love should be upon thy lips.

My Dear Little Boys,
At this hour I pray for guidance.
Remember love is important.
In the name of humanity,
Let me speak to your young hearts.

Boys,
Along life's journey,
There will be good and bad.
There should be no room for ignorance.

My Boys,
Follow the light.
Rise up and walk the good walk.
In the name of human dignity,
Remember to be humanlike.
Hide not your eyes from the fallen man.
Let your conscience dictate your path.

My Boys,
When this is done,
May history be kind to your names.

April 21, 2010

SO BE IT

My Boys,
When I heard of your growth,
My heart leapt for joy.
When I remember how David played up his harp just to please the
heart of his God,
I said to myself,
Who am I not to compose a song for my boys?
In deep meditation I find the sun.
From this heart I find my soul.
The use of this mind I set towards a higher power.
In peace and perfect love,
I pull from within a bundle of joy.

My Boys,
In this state of mind,
A song of love took a hold of my head.
At the Fountain of Love,
How could I not allow this heat to feed upon that which is good?

My Boys,
My music I cannot take with me.
May this hand find the rhythm it needs.
If I have to drink my tears,
So be it.
A song of love, I pray.

April 22, 2010

A MOMENT IN THE SUN

My Boys,
A moment in the sun,
Oh! What a wonderful morning!
Nature is in its glory.
Let me take time out to put my thoughts in order.
For the love of humanity,
Let me pray for peace and love.
The burden of man calls my spirit.
Who am I not to reason in the sun?
Now that my mind is fresh,
I shall give of myself.
A song of love I shall feed upon.
Man in his moment of madness,
I pray for the return of his rightful mind.

Blessed Father,
You are the great healer.
Today I call upon thee.
Remember your suffering children.
I have seen pain take hold of man,
That it pulls tears from the coldest of hearts.
Today I come before thee a broken man.
Let me live to see the working of thy hands.

April 24, 2010

THE SHARING OF LOVE

My Boys,
I took it upon myself to place love into your hearts.
I have lived a long life.
I have seen the behavior of man.
I have seen hatred parading its ugly face.
A whole nation cries out to a higher power.

Oh! Little Souls,
Forget not my hands.
I shall speak no evil thereof.

My Boys,
I am not a saint.
I am just a humble man doing my Father's work.

My Boys,
Remember the work must be done.

My Boys,
I give you my hands.
May history be kind to me.

April 29, 2010

GO IN PEACE

My Boys,
On this day the promises I dream of,
I shall keep.
Under the face of the sun,
A spirit of love I shall allow to grow.

My Boys,
I know what it means to walk in love.
Without love there will be no peace.
Well, then,
On this day I shall dedicate this hand.
Go in peace and do what is expected of you.

April 29, 2010

TENDER LOVE

My Boys,
When a man finds true love,
There is no burden too heavy to carry.
Your little tender love purified this heart.
The meaning of life took a different turn.
In the name of humanity,
Find that ambition to give back to society.

April 4, 2010

LEAD THE WAY

My Boys,
If the mind cannot feed upon love,
There will be no room for peace.
In my state of deep thinking,
Fond memories fuel the fire.

My Boys,
Keep the fire burning.
I am afraid of the dark.

Boys,
Lead the way and I shall follow.

May 4, 2010

WHAT SWEETNESS DO I TASTE?

My Boys,
What sweetness do I taste?
Sweet love I shall feed upon.
A song of love will be upon these lips.
The heart of the suffering man I shall seek.
Dripping tears I shall allow to take their course.
In the name of brotherly love,
I and I shall put this hand to good use.

My Boys,
A good deed is a must.
Harden not your hearts.
Live a life that others may follow.
Use your God-given talents to do that which is good.
In the name of mankind,
Rise up and let your voices be heard.
When this is done,
May history be kind to your young hands.

May 5, 2010

IF I SHOULD CRY

My God,
If I should cry,
Let me cry for peace and love.
I have seen man trading his soul for fine gold.
Yes, a fool will be a fool.
How long, my Lord, will this last?
When will man learn to be his brother's keeper?
Has he not eyes to see?
The earth closed its mouth upon what is left.

May 5, 2010

COME, MY BOYS

Come, my boys, look at a part of your roots.
In the name of human dignity,
This hand I shall leave to foster friendship.
Peace, my boys, I wish upon thee.
By the virtues of the elders,
Waste not your youth.
Seek and find the hearts of the Good Shepherds.
As for me,
I am on my journey.
How long could I not leave my marks for your young eyes?
The legacy of my father I pledge to honor.

My Boys, as I follow the stars,
Your faces I shall follow.
Let me pray.
Blessed Father, you have seen this heart.
May this hand be a guiding light for the boys.
Oh! Young souls remember to leave this world a better place.

May 5, 2010

MY BOYS, GO TELL IT

The power of love is the key.
My boys, go tell it.
A heart will never find happiness unless it feeds upon love.
My boys, strong love is the way to go.
My boys, at this moment in time,
I cannot find words to color the power of love.
I will only allow the heart to beat along.

Well, then, a song of love I shall sing along.
Today I stand before your young eyes.
Boys, I shall tell you no lies.
The power of love falls upon me.

May 6, 2010

A TRAIL OF LOVE

My Boys,
Your love leads me to a place of happiness.
Today I confine myself to nature.
My mind I allow to feed upon that which is good.
Before the sun escapes,
This hand I shall spare.

My Boys,
I shall listen to my music.
I will allow its rhythm to excite my heart.
In the name of pure love,
I shall sing along.

My Boys,
Great dreams I shall memorize,
Then allow these fingers to put them into words.
May I find a song of love to attract your young ears.
Let me pray.

Holy Father,
In your name I present these two boys.
May they understand my hands.

May 6, 2010

COME, MY LOVE

Oh! Love,
Take me to the eyes that I behold.
Who am I to turn away from the desire of this heart,
A heart that cannot rest?
Strong love I shall allow to take a stand.
In the name of true love,
I shall now call upon my spirit.
Take me.
Oh! Take me to where I belong.
Come, my love, let us break bread.

Friends of Mine,
Come rejoice with me.

May 7, 2010

THE RETURN OF MAN

Standing at the door of a fallen man,
Yes, I have seen man fallen from grace.
A mind that once fed upon that which is good,
Now pricks the brains of the great thinkers.
What is man?
What sadness have I seen?
How long, my Lord
How long, my Lord?
Where are thy hands?
Where is thy mercy?
How long shall I stand?
Blessed Father, if you are not too busy,
Let your hands be upon him.
Today I call upon thee.
Have mercy upon a fallen man.
Let him return to his rightful mind.
Awake, my spirit.
Awake, my spirit.
The return of man I pray.

May 9, 2010

MOTHER'S DAY POEM

Today I call upon every living soul.
Let us find the time to honor all Mothers.
Oh! What a precious gift to mankind.

Blessed Father,
In the name of true love,
Let every man be mindful to your creation.
Today we celebrate Mother's Day.
Grant us peace and love.
For those who have long gone,
May their souls rest in peace.

Oh! Mother,
How could I forget your tender hands?
In loving memory may your spirit never leave.
From the Fountain of Love may these tears cool this heart.
In the name of humanity,
I call upon my people.
In honor of our dear Mothers,
Rise up and let us give thanks.
We came from the dark to the light.
Now that we have seen the light,
May true love be our guide.

May 9, 2010

SWEET THOUGHTS

My Boys,
When a man finds love,
His thoughts will be sweet.
There will be no room for hatred.

My Boys,
Love will win over hatred.
Today I shall feed upon the love I received.

Oh! Divine Father,
You have seen the young hearts at work.
In the name of true love,
What purity I have seen.
Now the work must be done.
My life is full.

Blessed Father,
Help me to share the love.
What this world needs is true love.

Father,
I have seen the children leading the way.
Who am I not to follow?

May 10, 2010

VICTORY WEAPON

My Boys,
I have found my victory weapon.
Today I am on my journey.
For the good of man I cannot rest.
Time awaits no man.

My Boys,
Your light I have seen.
Blood to blood,
I shall go forth.
The streets of love I shall tread upon.
Now that my music is out,
I shall use these lips to move the words.
True love will be good for the quality of life.

My Boys,
I shall use this hand to spread the love.

Boys,
Love is the power to navigate you along the journey of life.
All that I am,
I shall share with you both.
I cannot sleep.
I have to entrap my ideas.
My mind and heart I have put forward.

May 11, 2010

A WORKING MIND

In the name of human dignity,
I shall use this mind to create a fountain of love.

Oh! People of Conscience,
Work with me.

Oh! Heavenly Father,
Let us feed upon thy love.
I have seen your children starving for love.
Where are the Good Shepherds?
Have I not eyes to see?
What purpose do I hold?
In the name of brotherly love,
I call upon my people to lend a hand.

My People,
Leave this place a better place.
Let each man give of himself.

My People,
There should be no room for hatred.
Life is short.
Let history be kind to you.
Today I come to you from the heart of suffering.
What pain I have seen.

My God,
How long shall I moan?
How long shall I hold the strain?
Where have all the good people gone?
Are they not in your book?

Father,
Who am I?
What am I?
Let my feet walk upon the streets of dignity.
A loving heart I pray to carry.

May 12, 2010

IN SILENCE

My Boys,
In silence I shall use this mind towards peace and love.
The both of you have shaped this heart.
Now that my soul is on fire,
A song of love I shall sing.
With a clear conscience,
I shall share the legacy.

My Friends,
In the name of true love,
I cannot hold my tongue.
Come rejoice with me.
Let us go to the Fountain of Love.

May 12, 2010

THE FACE OF HUMAN DIGNITY

My Boys,
In the face of human dignity,
I stand in the House of Human Suffering.
The morality of man.
I pray to find some good hands.
I have seen man in a state of suffering.
A mind that once captured the heart of good reasoning,
Now sheds its trademark.
What is man?
What pain I have seen.

Power Higher Than I,
Today I stand to face the rhythm.
Clear my mind I pray
For the good of man,
Here I am.

Blessed Father,
let me find the will to stand firm.
The work must be done.
Let me find the courage to lead.
Forget not your children.
The return of a great mind I pray.
If only I could find comforting words,
My day would be sweet.

May 18, 2010

IF ONLY EYES COULD TALK

Oh! Love,
Take me to the eyes of the weak hearts.

Blessed Father,
You have seen your children.
Eyes that were once clear as crystal,
Are now pulling from their sockets.

Father,
What shall I do?
Let not fear take a hold of me.
I came to this land for a purpose.
Who am I not to follow my calling?
Today I pray for a bold spirit.
The work must be done.
What rage I have seen.

Father,
I am too far gone.
In the name of human dignity,
I cannot turn back now.
The work must be done.

Father,
In your name I pray for your blessing.
Work with me that I may not be afraid.
Let me find the right words to calm their spirit.
Let me find the right tone of voice to deliver the message.

Father,
If you are with me,
Why should I be afraid?
Today I come to thee.
Oh! Take me along my journey.

May 20, 2010

A MIND GOING TO WASTE

A mind going to waste.

My People,
With these eyes I cannot leave.
When I look at man drifting to another phase,
I said to myself,
"Let me be thankful for a clear mind,
A mind that I shall use for the good of man."

My People,
In this state of deep reasoning,
The plight of man I wonder.

Oh! Great Healer,
You have seen what I have seen.
May your hands be upon the suffering man.
Today I call to thee in a state of raw emotions.
The working of the mind I do not understand,
Yet I cannot leave.

Oh! Great Teacher,
Teach me thy ways.
In the name of mankind,
Give unto us thy mercy.

Oh! Father of All Fathers,
Come to the aid of your children.
Only you can bring forth the keys.

Father,
Without the keys, we are nothing.
A sound mind I pray.

May 20, 2010

WHEN LOVE FINDS ITS PATH

My Dear,
When love finds its path,
No hatred will stand in its way.
What the world needs is love.
Nation against nation,
Man against man,
When will it end?
When will peace be upon the lips of man?
When will man find the will to be his brother's keeper?

My People,
Today I call upon all of God's children.
Let us go to the Fountain of Love.

My People,
A clean heart will be a blessing.
When this is done,
Go and do your Father's work.

May 20, 2010

SPIRITS AT PEACE

My Dear,
If I had not found the will to love,
At this hour my hands would be dead to picking words.
My heart would be drowning in tears.
Let me be thankful that our spirits are at peace.

My Dear,
My thoughts are at work.
In the name of peace,
Let us break bread.
In the name of true love,
May we call upon the father of love.
Life, my dear, will reach its end.
Let it not be said that a fool will always be a fool.
You have a mind of your own.
Set your conscience free,
Free from the weight of hatred,
Free from loose tongues.
Reach for the soul of humanity,
Then set your eyes upon the prize.
If a man cannot work to gain his wings,
He should not lay blame upon others.

My Dear,
Every man should find his purpose in life.
Today I shall allow this hand to speak for me.

May 21, 2010

A CHANGING FACE

What was once a face of steel is now at ease with a smile.
The good God must have washed away the dirt.
Oh! What a beautiful morning.
I smell peace and love.

Blessed Father,
Through you all things are possible.
Now that I am at ease,
Let me put my thoughts in order.
Today I shall pull from within.
May the child from within find a song of love.
Faces I know not,
Come to me.
Come let us reason.
In the name of humanity,
Let us find the will to love.

Blessed Father, the Teacher of All Love,
Here are your children.
Open your hearts that the power of love will find a place to grow.
Remove the pain from the faces I know not.
Today I have seen man in a state of shock.
From the lips hatred is eating away the heart.

Power Higher Than I,
Today I turn mine eyes t thee.
Remember these faces.

May 21, 2010

LITTLE BONFIRE

Come to me, my little bonfire.
Come and let me warm my spirit.
Come and let me fatten the eyes.
Awake, my spirit.
Awake, my spirit.
Today, today I shall stand before the fire I need.
Cold feet I do not need.

May 22, 2010

FRIENDSHIP

In the name of the Most High,
My friend, I come to thee.
Your pain shall be mine.
I cannot leave you now.
What conscience would I carry?
Well, then, my friend,
Let me speak.
What are friends for?
A true friend will share the pain and pleasure of life.
When a man is in need,
A true friend will lend a hand.

My Friend,
In the name of brotherhood,
I rise to serve thee.
Here are my hands.
Lean on me.

May 22, 2010

THE LIGHTS

The lights of mine eyes!
My friends, why should I worry?
Come rejoice with me.
What precious gift have I received?
Oh! Young souls,
Let me pray.

Blessed Father,
I have seen your handiwork.
In the eyes of man,
Man and boys found a common ground.
For the good of man,
May your hands be our guide.

May 25, 2010

MY THIRST

My Boys,
From the Fountain of Love I shall quench my thirst.
Your youthfulness brought me the fire I need.
Oh! Young eyes, leave me not.
The time is right for me to spread the words.

Boys,
In the name of true love,
Let me find words to adorn the Fountain of Love.

Boys,
Now that my spirit is right,
I shall preach nothing but love.

May 25, 2010

AN OPEN HEART

My Boys,
Now that I opened my heart to your young hearts,
May the God I serve be pleased.

My Boys,
With dignity I shall honor thee.
Let me be thankful I live to fatten mine eyes.

My Boys,
I have no time to lose.
The time is right for me to rejoice.
I shall wish upon the stars for long life.
For the good of man,
Take my hands to the eyes of man.

My Boys,
Remember when I am gone,
The work must continue.
Remember the spirits of the ancestors.
Remember their journey.
Remember their work towards human suffering.
When this is done,
Peace and love I wish upon your journey.

May 26, 2010

WHEN I AM ALONE

My Boys,
When I am alone,
Sweet words come to me like sweet dreams.
No journey will dampen my spirit.
A fresh mind will feed upon that which is good.

My Boys,
I will not hide my love.
A happy heart is in motion.
If I cannot teach the heart of true love,
Why should I live?
Well then, my boys,
I shall allow this hand to speak for me.
As I find the pleasure in nature,
I shall reach for my soul.
It's fine with me if I feed a child upon that which is good.
Such a child will produce that which is good.

Oh! Young Souls,
For the good of man I beg of you.
Find that dignity to serve.
Harden not your hearts.
Let not my teaching go to waste.
Let not the hands of the wicked find thee.

May 26, 2010

A TIME TO LEAVE

A time to leave...
My people, all good things must come to an end.
The Lord giveth and the Lord taketh.
Today I am upon the soil of my birth.
The love of my people fattens my heart,
Yet I shall leave for a far away land,
A home away from home.
From my father's land I shall spread the wealth to the heart of the
suffering man.
May I, the travelling man, follow my father's dream.
Oh! Great Father, the Father of all fathers,
Here I am training my thoughts towards humanity.

May 26, 2010

DREAMING

My Boys,
How can I stop dreaming?
Dreams upon dreams I have stored.
In the name of humanity I shall allow destiny to lead me to my
destination.
My purpose in life I shall allow words to shape my path.

Oh! Good Shepherds,
Leave me not.
Have I not eyes to see the fall of man?
Boasting lips are now covered with shame.

Oh! Great Dreams,
Your path I shall follow.
For the good of man I shall dream along.
Today I have allowed my music to play.

My Boys,
Today I pray that your feet find the rhythm.

May 28, 2010

MY WORK

When a man finds time to work his thoughts,
The soul of humanity should be upon him.
Man in a state of suffering should not escape the eyes.

My People,
I call upon every man to leave this world a better place.
Today I took time out to be with nature.
The sun I cannot escape.
The heavens I can see clearly.

Blessed Father,
If I am in thy sight,
Point me to the rock that is higher than I.
Let my work speak for me.
The things I want to do,
Let me find the will to use this hand.

Oh! Mighty One,
Here I am.
My shadow and I cry out to thee.
The face of the suffering man I present to thee.

Blessed Father,
Only you can show him the way.
Spur him that he may gallop with good strap to his back.

May 28, 2010

LEAVE SOMETHING GOOD

You came to this world to represent mankind.
Let it not be said that you have failed the heart of man.
Let history be kind to your years.
Let your name be upon the lips of others.
A good man will receive his wings.

My People,
Waste not your stay upon this land.
Leave something good for mankind.

May 28, 2010

IN LINE OF DUTY

My Dear,
In line of duty,
There will be no rest for our seeing eyes.
All eyes are upon us.

My Dear,
Duty and only duty shall be our cry.
In the name of human dignity,
Rise up to do a good deed.
In the name of the Father,
Let us follow the path of the Good Shepherds.
Today I shall call upon you.
Bring forth the good from within.

Oh! Heavenly Father,
You have seen the task ahead.
What darkness fell upon us.
What pity pulls our hearts.
In the name of human suffering,
Grant us the understanding to do that which is good.

Father,
Within our sights,
The burden of man penetrates the soul.
Now that I stand face to face,
Father, lift up our spirits.
Where there is darkness,
Let the light shine.

My God,
Today I cannot stand my heels.
The work must be done.

June 10, 2010

LOVE SPEAKS

My Boys,
Love speaks to a man who is right.
This troubled world needs love.
A man fitted with love will follow the teaching of the great Father.

My Lord,
In the name of peace and love,
Today I come to thee.
Fill me up that I may share the legacy.
What this world needs is love.
I have seen hatred jumping like maggots,
Nation against nation,
Son against father,
Daughter against mother,
Friends against friends.

My God,
When will it end?

Father of All Love,
Teach us the ways.
Soften our hearts that man will find the will to love.

June 10, 2010